BASIC ENGLISH SERIES

Drama 1

The **Basic English Series** consists of:

Poetry 1, 2 and 3
Story 1, 2 and 3
Drama 1, 2 and 3
Language 1, 2 and 3

BASIC ENGLISH SERIES

Drama 1

John L. Foster

Macmillan Education

Selection and Activities © John L. Foster 1987
Voices © Gareth Owen
How Green You Are! © Berlie Doherty
Finders Keepers © David Williams
Up School © David Foxton
Whiteghosts © Tony Coult

First published 1987

Published by
MACMILLAN EDUCATION LTD
Houndmills, Basingstoke, Hampshire RG21 2XS
and London
Companies and representatives
throughout the world

Designed by Linda Reed
Illustrated by Ann Gowland, Pat Tyler and Anna Hancock

Printed in Hong Kong

British Library Cataloguing in Publication Data
Foster, John L. (John Louis)
Drama 1. — (Basic English series)
1. children's plays, English
I. Title   II. Series
822′.914′0809282   PR1259.J8
ISBN 0−333−41574−4

Contents

Acknowledgement

How Green You Are! was first published in novel form as chapter 1 of *How Green You Are!* by Berlie Doherty, published by Methuen Children's Books.

1: Voices

GARETH OWEN

The characters

TERRY GREENFIELD
ANITA, his cousin
GRAN
TASKER, a bully
DUCKETT, his mate
BRON, his mate
MISS DIAMOND, a Headmistress
MISS TOWNSEND, a Teacher
MR HEARD, a Teacher
SANDRA
A BOY
CHILD 1
CHILD 2
CHILD 3
A CLASS
AN ASSEMBLY

SCENE 1: (*Music. Over the music we hear Terry's voice talking quietly. The music continues over.*)

Terry: I suppose it was because I was small for my age that he picked on me. That and the fact that I wore glasses. Tasker was in the class above me and he was big. Really big. I didn't have a chance. Anyway he always had his mates with him, Duckett and Bron. He wasn't taking any chances. No matter how I tried to avoid them, they were always there. Being a victim can become a habit. I think Tasker knew that.

(*Sound of playground. Footsteps.*)

It became a habit for him too. You could almost say he needed me.

Tasker: Look what the tide dragged up.

Duckett: What is it?

Bron: Where is it, you mean. (*Laughter.*)

Tasker: It's my friend Terry.

Terry: Shut up, Tasker.

Duckett: It's not very polite, Task. Not very polite whatever it is.

Bron: It's an ant.

Duckett: A four-eyed ant.

Tasker: It's a pygmy.

Duckett: A four-eyed pygmy.

Terry: Leave me alone, Tasker.

Tasker: What if I don't, Pygmy? What you gonna do about it? You gonna hit me, are you? Gonna hit me; like that?

(*Sound of a blow. Terry falls.*)

Tasker: Oh look, he's fallen down.

Terry: Geroff me.

Duckett: He fell down on the floor.

Tasker: Must have been 'cos his head hit my fist.

(*Sound of spectacles falling to the floor.*)

Duckett: Look at this, Task.

Tasker: His glasses.

Terry: Give them here.

Tasker: Let me try.

Duckett: Smart.

Tasker: Can't see nothing. You must be half-blind, Pygmy.

Terry: Give them back.

Tasker: Naughty. Shouldn't snatch.

(*Sound of glasses breaking.*)

Tasker: Oh, look at that.

Duckett: You was careless there, Task.

Terry: You broke my glasses.

Tasker: What an unfortunate accident. They fell under my foot.

Bron: What a shame.

Tasker: Yeah, very unfortunate. Cost quite a bit to get them fixed. Want to make a contribution, Pygmy?

Duckett: Quid any good, Task?

Tasker: Shouldn't think so. Looks like an expensive job to me.

Terry: That's my money.

Bron: Let's have a look in these other pockets.

Duckett: All he's got, Task.

Tasker: Have to do, won't it?

Terry: You better give that back . . .

Tasker: Or what, Pygmy? Now if anybody asks you, be sure to tell 'em it was an accident. 'Cos if you don't, you know what'll happen. Know what I mean? Yeah, I think you do. I think you do.

(*Sound of radio weather forecast. Sound of a key in the lock and front door closing. We are in Terry's grandmother's house.*)

Terry: Gran! Gran it's me. Terry.

Gran: Who's that?

Terry: It's me, Gran. (*Aside*) Come on up, she's in the bedroom.

Gran: Is that you, Terry? Come on up.

Terry: Hello Gran. Mum sent you some lemon cheese.

Gran: That's nice. Let me turn the Weather off.

(*The radio is switched off.*)

I like to listen to the Weather. Who's the girl you've got with you?

Anita: It's me, Anita.

Terry: You know, my cousin.

Gran: Haven't seen you. Haven't seen anybody for ten years.

Anita: How did you know I was a girl?

Gran: I can tell things like that. Blind people often can.

Terry: Gran can tell it's me by the way I open the door.

Gran: Come closer here, Anita love. Blonde hair. You've got blonde hair.

Terry: She has too.

Anita: That's amazing. That you can tell.

Gran: Not really.

Terry: Gran used to be able to read the future.

Anita: The future?

Terry: In the tea cups. Couldn't you, Gran? She'd look at the leaves and tell you what was going to happen to you.

Anita: I don't know if I'd like that.

Gran: Only the good things, love. It's terrible if you see bad news. When my Frank passed on, I knew. I saw it there clear as day. I couldn't tell him. But I know. It was a burden. Terrible.

Terry: Frank was Gran's husband.

Gran: Gone fifteen years now. But I remember it as clear as .... How old are you, love?

Anita: Fourteen.

Gran: A year older than Terry.

Terry: She's in the class above me.

Gran: That's nice. Yes, remember him like it was yesterday. Poor Frank. Oh he suffered. I spoke to him this morning.

Anita: This morning? But I thought . . . .

Gran: His spirit, dear, his spirit. He doesn't come to see me every day. But if I need some help he comes to me. It's a comfort. Some people think I'm a crank. I don't mind. They can think what they like. Would you like a chocolate, dear? Yes, those are nice. I like the nougat. There's a lot of people here. I talk to them all.

Anita: Where?

Gran: You can't see them, love. But they're here all the same. Being blind helps. I feel their presence.

Anita: Oooh.

Gran: Did I frighten you? I didn't mean to frighten you. They're like memories really. That's what they are. Some people might call them ghosts. I call them memories. *You* sometimes think of people when they're not there, don't you?

Anita: I suppose so.

Gran: There you are then. That's what I call ghosts. The people in my past life. If I'm lonely I call them to me. They usually come. Terry, get my purse, there's a good lad.

Anita: I'd be scared stiff to be in the dark all the time. I hate the dark.

Gran: You get used to it, love.

Terry: Can't find it, Gran.

Gran: Where's your glasses?

Terry: Glasses?

Gran: You've broke them, haven't you?

Terry: How did you know?

Gran: Come over here. Come here. Give me your hand.
What are you scared of?

Terry: Scared?

Gran: Somebody's scaring you. What is it?

Terry: It's nothing.

Gran: You can tell your Gran. You're in trouble, aren't you?
One of your teachers, is it?

Terry: Nobody's scaring me.

Anita: Mrs Greenfield . . . .

Terry: Shut up, Anita. You say anything . . .

Gran: What is it?

Terry: Nothing, Gran. Your purse must be downstairs. I'll
fetch it.

(*He goes down the stairs. We hear his footsteps descending. Then
his voice further off.*)

Terry: I'll fetch it.

Gran: Anita.

Anita: Yes.

Gran: Come here. I knew your dad, you know. He had fair
hair too. Always in trouble. Now. What's up with our Terry?

Anita: Well, I don't know . . .

Gran: Tell me. Somebody knocking him about, is there?

Anita: Well, yes. A boy at school.

Gran: What's his name?

Anita: Tasker. Billy Tasker. He's older than Terry. He's in my class. They broke Terry's glasses. They're always waiting for him.

Gran: Why won't he tell his Dad?

Anita: Frightened to. He knows Tasker'll get back at him.

Gran: If I could get hold of him I'd give him what for.

Anita: Don't tell him I said anything.

(*Sound of footsteps. Terry entering.*)

Gran: That's it, Terry. Let's have a look.
Now there's five pounds. You take the purse, you see. Now I want a loaf. A large one. And some of those lardy cakes from Jackson's. Packet of tea. Not bags. Pound of butter. That's it. Oh and get me a copy of *The Argus*. Tomorrow will do.

Terry: I have to go, Gran.

Gran: That's right.

Anita: Bye, Mrs Greenfield.

Gran: Bye, love. Come and see me again. Oh, and Terry. About what's worrying you.

Terry: It's nothing.

Gran: I'll have a think about it. I'll have a word with Frank, he'll come up with something.

Terry: Bye, Gran.

Gran: And don't forget *The Argus*. I'll want you to read me the deaths column tomorrow.

(*Her voice fades as the front door closes.*)

Gran: I enjoy a good read of the deaths column.

(*School Assembly. Hymn singing. It stops. Shuffling of feet. Coughing. Miss Diamond, the Head, is addressing the School.*)

Miss Diamond: Stop that coughing. It's more like a hospital than a school. Are you ready, Fowler? Well, look this way. Now, as I'm sure you know, and if you don't you should, next week is a very important date in the history of St Phillip's, in the history of the school. It will be our hundredth anniversary. That's older than most of us here, isn't it? Even than some of the teachers.

(*Laughter, coughing, shuffling.*)

Miss Diamond: Now then, to celebrate this special birthday, we're holding an Open Day to which past pupils, parents and a number of other very important people will be invited. In addition to your work, the normal kind of thing that we put on show on Open Days, there'll be an exhibition recording the history of your school. Your class teachers will explain in more detail. But while we're all here together I wanted you to think what a hundred years means. Think of all the children who have stood as you are standing now, in this hall. Many of them lived to a great age. Many died in two terrible wars. But you can't help but feel their presence about you. I want you to think about what they might have been like. How things have changed over the years. Will you do that over the next fortnight? Good.

Now I've two names on my list. Two people who've spoiled things again for everybody else. Tasker? Tasker.

Tasker: Yes.

Miss Diamond: Yes, Miss Diamond.

Tasker: Yes, Miss Diamond.

Miss Diamond: And Greenfield.

Terry: Yes, Miss Diamond.

Miss Diamond: Outside my office, both of you.
Ready, Miss Townsend?
First forms file out quietly, please.

(*Piano pumps out a march. Some talking and sound of feet.*)

Miss Diamond: Tasker, Greenfield; inside.

(*The door closes. The piano is fainter now and finally stops.*)

Miss Diamond: Now then Tasker, what's all this about?

Tasker: What's what about, Miss?

Miss Diamond: Are we going to have to go through all this? Bewildered innocence. Come along, Tasker. We know each other too well. Why do you think I asked you here? Do you think it's because I enjoy your company?

Tasker: Dunno, Miss.

Miss Diamond: D'you take me for a fool, Tasker? Do you?

Tasker: No, Miss.

Miss Diamond: I'm not so sure. Mr Miller says he found the two of you climbing and fighting on the Fraser Street wall. Are you saying you weren't there? Are you saying that Mr Miller is a liar?

Tasker: No, Miss.

Miss Diamond: So you were there?

Tasker: } Yes, Miss.
Terry: }

Miss Diamond: So you do know what I'm talking about? Now, can you tell me why you were climbing over the wall instead of coming through the main gate like everybody else?

Tasker: I was late for school, Miss. If I'd gone round I'd have been late.

Miss Diamond: But Mr Miller saw you at 8.30 this morning. You couldn't have been late. And if you're going to roll off the wall I wish you'd have the decency to fall on to the school side where nobody could see you . . . I don't know. What have you to say, Greenfield?

Terry: Nothing, Miss.

Miss Diamond: Nothing. And what about this purse Mr Miller found? Looks like a shopping list. Is that your handwriting, Greenfield?

Terry: No, Miss.

Miss Diamond: Mmh. A shopping list that adds up to nearly five pounds. But there's no five pounds. Can you explain that, Tasker?

Tasker: Don't know anything about it, Miss.

Miss Diamond: Of course you don't. And what's this about your not being able to do your writing because your glasses were smashed. How did they get smashed?

Terry: Fell, Miss.

Head: You fell. Now, look, Tasker, if there's been bullying going on; if five pounds have been stolen; let me spell it out very clearly. That is a crime. A crime, Tasker. And the police will have to be called. Do you understand that? Now Greenfield, if Tasker has been bullying it's your duty to tell me. I don't want you protecting him. So I'll ask you once more . . . .

(*Sound of door opening.*)

Miss Townsend: Excuse me, Miss Diamond.

Miss Diamond: What is it, Miss Townsend?

Miss Townsend: You wanted to look at the new PE mats before we began.

Miss Diamond: Thank you, Miss Townsend. I'll be there right away. You two think about what I've said. I'll be expecting an answer.

(*Sound of her footsteps exiting.*)

Tasker: (*Whispering.*) Listen, Pygmy. I hope you're thinking very hard about what you're going to say.

Terry: Give it back. That was my Gran's, that five pounds.

Tasker: Ah no. It *was*. Now it's mine.

Terry: If you don't give it back, I'll tell her.

Tasker: No you won't, Four Eyes. You won't say anything. And I'll tell you why. Because I'll be there. Waiting for you. You thought you'd escape me, coming in early this morning. Didn't make no difference. I'll be there. Wherever you go. So what you'll tell Diamond is that you've never seen that purse. Understand?

Terry: No, I'll . . .

Tasker: Understand? (*The sound of a blow.*)
And you won't say nothing about your specs neither.
Understand? (*Another blow*).

(*Sound of door opening. Miss Diamond enters.*)

Miss Diamond: Well, Greenfield. What are you going to tell
me?

Terry: Miss.

Miss Diamond: Shall I tell you what I think? I think Tasker
took this purse off you. You were doing messages and he
stole it. Isn't that true? Tasker? Well, isn't it?

Tasker: No, Miss. Ask him, Miss.

Miss Diamond: Well, Greenfield?

Terry: No, Miss.

Miss Diamond: Look at me, Terry. This purse. It's yours, isn't
it? Tasker took the money out of it, didn't he? Well? (*Pause*)
Didn't he?

Terry: No, Miss.

Miss Diamond: Are you sure?

Terry: I've never seen the purse before, Miss.

Miss Diamond: I don't know. I really don't know. Go to your
classrooms.

(*Sound of chatter. A class discussion going on. Not unruly.*)

Mr Heard: All right, simmer down. Listen, listen. All right,
you three groups know what you're going to do. How about
you lot?

Sandra: Sir, sir.

Mr Heard: Sandra.

Sandra: Sir, I'm going to go round, like, all the people who was here, sir, and ask them for any photos they got when they was, like, young, sir, you know, when they was at the school, sir, and then I'd take their picture as they are now, sir, and put them up together, like, side by side.

Mr Heard: Sounds like a good plan. But remember to be a bit diplomatic and tell them what you're going to do. Some people don't like to be reminded of how old they've got. (*Pause.*) Good, yes. Anybody else in that group? Anita?

Anita: I thought what I could do, sir, was I'd ask lots of old people what the school was like years ago and put it all on a tape recorder. Like what they remember.

Mr Heard: Anyone in mind?

Anita: Terry's grandmother, sir.

Mr Heard: Terry?

Anita: My cousin, sir. He's in 2A, sir. But his grandmother's, like, she's blind, sir, but she's got a really good memory, sir, and she's dead old.

Mr Heard: As long as she's not old and dead.

Class: Ooooer.

Anita: Sir! She tells ghost stories. About people she remembers. She says they're like ghosts to her, sir, and they come back and she speaks to them.

Mr Heard: Fair enough. I've heard quite a few people say the school's haunted.

Class: Sir! Ooooh.

Mr Heard: All right, that'll do. Or I'll make ghosts of some of you.

(*Sound of door opening.*)

Ah, Tasker. Talking of ghosts. Where have you been till now? Kind of you to grace us with your presence.

Tasker: Had to see Miss Diamond, sir.

Mr Heard: Don't tell me. She wants you to be Head Boy. No, no she wants you to be a brain surgeon.

Boy: And operate on himself.

(*Laughter.*)

Tasker: I'll get you, Smethurst.

Mr Heard: That's enough. Tasker, you go in that group with Anita and Sandra and Darrell.

Sandra: Oh sir!

Mr Heard: We were talking about memories and ghosts.

Tasker: Boring, sir.

Mr Heard: Yes, I know you are, Tasker, but just do your best. Fine, work on your own in those groups . . . (*His voice begins to fade.*) and I'll want to hear a rough outline by, let's say, 10.30.

(*Sound of a key in a lock.*)

Terry: Come on in.

Anita: Will she be in?

Terry: She sleeps in the afternoon. She sleeps a lot.

(*Sound of door closing.*)

Come in the kitchen, I'll make her a pot of tea.

Anita: You going to tell her?

(*Sounds of tea being made. Cupboards opened and shut. Water running. Gas lit. Crockery.*)

Terry: Tell her what?

Anita: You know. About the purse and the money and everything.

Terry: Dunno. Later, maybe.

Anita: You have to tell her, stupid. She's going to find out some time. What are you going to say when she finds out you haven't brought her messages?

Terry: I'll think of something.

Anita: Why didn't you tell Miss Diamond?

Terry: He'd murder me.

Anita: Tasker?

Terry: Yeah.

Anita: You can't let it drag on. He picks on you because you don't do anything about it. What's so good about being beaten up all the time?

Terry: Pass the sugar.

Anita: Perhaps you could hide somewhere. Where he couldn't find you.

Terry: Like Alaska.

Anita: Mmh. Perhaps you'll grow.

Terry: What, like ten inches overnight.

Anita: Take one of them body-building courses.

Terry: You have to have a body to start with.

Anita: Perhaps your Gran could make a model of him and stick needles through his brain.

Terry: What brain?

Anita: Or haunt him. Oooooooh.

Terry: Gerroff. Here, d'you think there are . . . you know?

Anita: Ghosts?

Terry: Yeah.

Anita: Hope not.

Terry: Rather have a ghost than Tasker.

Anita: You know when he came back to our class after you'd been with him?

Terry: To see Miss Diamond.

Anita: Yeah. He was in our group and we were like talking about ghosts and all that, you know. Like, I didn't say it was your Gran. Well, he made fun like, said it was all rubbish. But, well he didn't like it. I could tell. So I went on about the school being haunted, like Mr Heard said. He didn't like it. Went quiet. He kept joking. But he was joking because he didn't like it all.

Terry: Gran's only talking to herself really. She's lonely, that's all.

Anita: My Auntie talks to her dog.

Terry: What's funny about that? Everybody talks to their dog.

Anita: This one's been dead about twenty years.

Terry: Let's take this tea up to Gran.

Anita: It got run over by an ice cream van in Mafeking Terrace.

Terry: That's nice.

Anita: She keeps going out in the garden and calling him, 'Xeno, Xeno, nice din din.'

Terry: Xeno?

Anita: Puts food out for him.

Terry: Perhaps the ghost of Xeno haunts the garden.

Anita: She has a cat now.

Terry: Must be confused.

Anita: Half the time he thinks he's an alsatian called Xeno.

(*Sound of door opening.*)

Terry: Gran.

Gran: Oh!

Terry: Still asleep?

Gran: What? No, just closed me eyes for a few minutes. Thought it was you.

Terry: Made you some tea.

Gran: You're a good boy. Anita's with you, isn't she?

Anita: I'm here, Mrs Greenfield.

Gran: Did you get them, Terry?

Terry: What's that, Gran?

Gran: You know, the messages. I gave you money for messages.

Terry: Oh yeah.

Gran: Where are they?

Terry: Oh yeah. They're downstairs. You want me to fetch them up?

Gran: All right. No, leave it. Have you got my change?

Terry: Change?

Gran: I gave you five pounds.

Terry: Oh yeah. No, there wasn't any change.

Gran: From five pounds? Well I never. There must have been.

Terry: Oh yes, I forgot, there was. But I left it at home. I had to go home. I changed my trousers. Got the paper, though. Gran, Anita wanted to ask you something.

Gran: Me?

Anita: Yes, Mrs Greenfield. You see we're doing a project at school.

Gran: What's that when it's at home?

Anita: It's all about the history of St Phillip's. Like it's a hundred years old this month, you see, and we all have to find out something different. So what I decided to do was, well, you were at St Phillip's, weren't you?

Gran: And my mother. That's Terry's great-great-granny. I can remember her taking me to school the first day.

Anita: That's what I'd like you to talk about and I've brought my tape recorder. I wondered if you'd mind me taking it all down.

Gran: Tape recorder?

Anita: You just tell me about what you remember. Anything at all and the machine records it.

Gran: I see. Shall I start now?

Anita: Just a minute . . .

Gran: Let me see . . . .

Anita: And I'll plug this in. All right here?

Gran: Of course it was just the Elementary School then. Just the one building . . .

Anita: Just a minute . . . .

(*We hear her throughout this exchange setting up her tape recorder.*)

That's it, I'm ready.

Gran: What d'you want me to say?

Anita: Anything you remember. Mr Heard told us this morning that the school's haunted.

Gran: That's right.

Anita: You mean real ghosts?

Gran: Oh yes, of course.

Anita: Did you ever see them?

Gran: Not see them, no, but .... It was after the burning, you see.

Anita: The school was burnt?

Gran: Oh yes, completely. It was terrible. Hadn't been opened long. That was in my mother's day, that was. That's not the same school. It's different, is that. It were right small when my Mam was there. Two classes, that's all. She had the measles that day, otherwise she'd have gone too.

Terry: Gone?

Gran: They thought she might die of it, the measles. Kept her at home, you see. It was a blessing in disguise.

Anita: And all the other children died?

(*Sound of music, soft and moody creeps in.*)

Gran: Every last child. It was a tragedy. Small village then, d'you see. Nearly every street lost a child. Terrible it was.

Anita: But what about the ghosts?

Gran: Mam, she could remember every name. Every name of every poor, dead burnt child. Well she knew them, of course. Saw them every day. You would remember that. She still thought of them as young, you see. Sixty years after, she could remember every last name. Every one. She could recite them. Tell me what each one of them looked like. She passed them on to me. I suppose it was her way of keeping them alive. Like a monument in a way. All the names. Ninety-odd years dead.
Eileen Allynson, Dora Bradley, Tommy Costigan ....

Anita: But you say that you ... You didn't see them?

Gran: Oh yes. They're still there. All around me. They mustn't be forgotten. Never. I bring them back, you see. Yes, I bring them all back.

Anita: But if you didn't see them, how . . . ?

Gran: Heard them. Heard their voices.

Anita: Of all the dead children?

Gran: I'd be about thirteen, going on fourteen. About your age, d'you see. We lived in Temple Street. It was a village then. I'd gone over to see Uncle John in Melrose Street. It's a housing estate now. Nearly all fields then. He had a little tobacconist's shop. He wasn't well. Hadn't been well, you see. I took over some food for him. The clock must have stopped. I missed the bus. Missed the bus and I had to walk. Through the fields there was a lane, a short cut, like. It went by the school. I thought, I'll cut across through the school. It was late then. Nobody about, not a soul. Going round the school wall, I smelled something. It was like a burning smell. I looked towards the school where the smell came from. There were no flames. Nothing. I climbed the wall. I went towards the classroom. I went over. Just the darkness. Then . . .

(*Sound of a huge fire cuts in.*)

I heard it. Like a great fire. But no flames. No flames at all. Then there was the voice. In the black I heard a voice. Then another. Like children's voices calling out their names. Calling out their names. I couldn't understand. I didn't know the names. But I'd heard them. There was something about them. Then I remembered; they were the names my mother recited. It was like a poem, a long sad poem made up of names. Voices out of the dead past. I ran home. I ran all the way home. And all the way I could still hear them. I could never tell whether they were in the air or in my head. All those names. Eileen Allynson, Dora Bradley, Tommy Costigan, Denise Chandler, Alan Delaney, Paula Delaney, Joanna Ellison . . .

(As she recites, the voices of individual children begin to recite with her. Almost inaudible at first but then gathering in volume while at the same time her voice fades away.)

Hannah Everitt
Emma Farmer
Peter Farrell
Daniel Garrett
Daisy Hammond
Phillip Ince
Madeline Ingoldsby
Daniel Kennedy
Robert Lund
Annie Price
Avril Summers

(A short silence.)

Miss Townsend: Good. That came out very clearly, didn't it, Class 2?

All: Yes, Miss.

Miss Townsend: Is that what you wanted, Anita, Terry?

Anita: Yes, Miss.

Miss Townsend: How did it make you feel, Class 2, recording all those names?

Child 1: Funny, Miss.

Child 2: Creepy, Miss.

Child 3: Yeah, funny, Miss. Like they're all dead, Miss. They're all dead people's names.

Miss Townsend: That's right, Sarah. They're ghosts, aren't they?

Class: Yes, Miss.

Miss Townsend: What are you going to do with it now, Anita?

Anita: I've got a recording of Mrs Greenfield.

Terry: That's my Gran, Miss.

Anita: Yes, Miss, I've got her on my tape recorder, like, talking about the olden days. She tells this ghost story. So at the beginning and the end I'll put these names.

Miss Townsend: Good idea.
Well thank you, Anita, you'd better be getting back to your own class now. Do you want some help with that machine?

Terry: I'll help her, Miss.

Miss Townsend: All right Terry, but don't be long.

Anita: Thanks for letting me do it here, Miss. I couldn't do it in my class because . . .

Miss Townsend: You wanted it to be a surprise.

Anita: Yes, Miss.

Miss Townsend: Well, someone open the door for them.

(*Sound of door and footsteps.*)

Miss Townsend: Now let's look again at the question of this decimal point. Angela, you come out and show me . . . .

(*Her voice fades as the door closes and Anita and Terry walk down the corridor. They whisper.*)

Terry: What do you think?

Anita: Sounds good.

Terry: It's brilliant. When shall we do it?

Anita: What?

Terry: You know.

Anita: I don't know.

Terry: You backing out?

Anita: Course not.

Terry: It was you who kept telling me to do something about Tasker. Well, I'm doing it.

Anita: Do I have to come here at midnight?

Terry: No point if you don't.

Anita: I'll be on my own.

Terry: You promised.

Anita: What if Dad won't let me out?

Terry: You wait till they're asleep. Creep out.

Anita: They don't go to bed till half past eleven.

Terry: Make it one, then.

Anita: How do I get into school?

Terry: Through the boiler room. It comes out in the corridor near the hall. I'll leave it open this afternoon. It's dead easy.

Anita: Like sailing the Atlantic on a doughnut.

Terry: You promised.

Anita: What about the tape recorder? I can't climb over the wall with that.

Terry: You leave it here. You leave it in your classroom all ready. All you have to do is switch it on.

Anita: How will you get out?

Terry: I'll stay at Gran's. I often do. It'll be easy. She takes a sleeping pill every night.

Anita: What if Tasker won't do it?

Terry: He will. If I ask him in front of his mates.

Anita: But what if he doesn't?

Terry: I don't know. We'd have to think of something else. If this works, he won't pick on me again. He wouldn't dare, or we'd tell the whole school. Well?

Anita: I hate the dark. I could die of fright. I read about this man who waited in a room to see a ghost. In the morning his hair had turned white.

Terry: Can't happen to you. You're blonde already.

Anita: Could go bald. How will I know when to switch it on?

Terry: I'll say something. Give a signal. Like a whistle.

Anita: Whistle?

Terry: Like an owl. Like this.

(*He makes a soft, owl-like whistle.*)

Miss Diamond: What are you two doing out here in the corridor?

Anita: Just going to my classroom, Miss.

Miss Diamond: What's all this whistling about?

Terry: It was an owl, Miss.

Miss Diamond: An owl?

Terry: For a play we're doing.

Miss Diamond: Is it indeed?

Terry: It's a sort of signal. A kind of signal, that's all.

(*Sounds of the playground fade in as Terry's voice fades out.*)

Tasker: Shoot, shoot.

Duckett: Over here.

Tasker: It's Tasker with the ball. Shoots.

Duckett: Unlucky, Task.

Bron: Couldn't even beat a blind Pygmy.

Tasker: Come here you, goalie.

Terry: When you going to give me my five pounds?

Tasker: I don't know nothing about no five pounds. Think of it as an extended loan.

Terry: Extended loan?

Tasker: Yeah. Like for ever.

Terry: If you don't give it back, something could happen to you.

Tasker: Oh yeah. Like what?

Terry: That was my Granny's fiver.

Tasker: That's the witch, innit? Here Duck, Four Eyes's Granny's a witch.

Terry: You better be careful what you say.

Duckett: She'll turn you into a frog, Task.

Tasker: Shurrup.

Duckett: Come on.

Tasker: Just a minute. We was like talking. Like Anita she was saying. She had this recording, your Granny what's a witch, saying she heard these kids. These dead kids who came back.

Terry: Yeah.

Tasker: You believe that?

Terry: I believe it. I heard them.

Tasker: You? Gerraway.

Terry: Last year. I came back. Came past one night. I heard them all.

Tasker: Gerraway. You're having me on.

Terry: Suit yourself.

Tasker: You heard them?

Terry: Sure. D'you want to?

Tasker: What?

Terry: Come with me. Come back here.

Tasker: What? At night?

Terry: Unless you're scared.

Duckett: Come on Task, ain't you playing?

Tasker: Four Eyes here wants me to come and find some ghosts.

Terry: Only he's too scared.

Tasker: Listen, Runt.

Duckett: It's cobblers.

Tasker: Yeah, cobblers.

Terry: So you'll come back.

Tasker: What? Yeah all right, we'll come.

Terry: Not them. Just you and me. They can come to the school gate. Just me and him go in.

Tasker: Not Duck and Bron?

Terry: Unless you're too scared without them.

Tasker: Me? It's just a story, innit?

Terry: Tonight then?

Tasker: Tonight?

Terry: Why not? It's the anniversary of the fire.

Tasker: I don't reckon there was no fire.

Duckett: You ain't scared are you, Task?

Tasker: Got to be joking.

Terry: Tonight then.

Tasker: All right. Why not?

Terry: See you here. By the gates. About ten to one.

Tasker: Fair enough.

Duckett: Come on, Task. Ain't you playing?

Tasker: Yeah, I'm playing. Quarter to one then. You better be there.

Terry: I'll be there, all right. Don't you worry. I'll be there.

(*Music softly. A clock strikes the quarters. Dog barks distantly. Footsteps.*)

Bron: (*Whispering*) What's that?

Duckett: Ssh.

Tasker: Someone.

Terry: Tasker?

Duckett: It's the Pygmy.

Tasker: Didn't think he'd have the bottle.

Terry: Who's with you?

Tasker: Bron, Duck.

Terry: They're not coming in.

Tasker: Course not.

Terry: Just you and me.

Duckett: What's that?

Bron: Only a dog.

Tasker: You going to be all right, Duck? Without me to hold your hand?

Duckett: Shurrup.

Tasker: Come on.

Bron: Here, bring a ghost back for me.

Tasker: See you.

(*Footsteps and rustling.*)

Terry: Down here.

Tasker: Gate's locked.

Terry: Under this wire.

Tasker: How do we get in?

Terry: Through the boiler room. I left it open.

Tasker: What's that?

Terry: Ssh.

Tasker: Copper.

Terry: In here.

(*Pause. Footsteps.*)

Terry: He's going the other way. Come on.

(*Sound of door creaking open.*)

Tasker: Dark in here.

Terry: You want to go back?

Tasker: Leave it out. Where are you? Ouch.

Terry: Over here.

Tasker: Bleeding head.

Terry: What's that?

Tasker: What?

Terry: Listen.

(*Silence.*)

Terry: Thought I heard something. Come on.

Tasker: You believe that story? The fire.

Terry: Up these stairs.

Tasker: Funny about the fire.

Terry: Fire?

Tasker: In the school. Asked me dad. He remembered hearing about it.

Terry: Leave the door.

Tasker: Where are we?

Terry: Come on. Here's the hall.

Tasker: Can you see in the dark?

Terry: I'm used to not being able to see. Without my glasses.

Tasker: Funny at night.

Terry: The stage.

Tasker: This where they are?

(*Clock strikes.*)

Terry: That classroom.

(*Silence. Their breathing.*)

Tasker: Nothing. Come on, let's go.

Terry: Listen.

Tasker: What?

Terry: Crackling. You hear it?

Tasker: What is it?

Terry: Owls flying.

Tasker: Owls?

Terry: Whoooo whooooo.

Tasker: Shut up.

(*We hear the first name in the distance. The voices gradually increase in volume. They overlap the dialogue thus:*)

                                          Eileen Allynson

Terry: Listen.

Tasker: What?   Paula Delaney

Terry: Over there.

Tasker: Where?

Terry: You hear it?   Joanna Ellison

Tasker: Yeah.

Terry: The voices.

Tasker: Them.

                                          Hannah Everitt

(*The voices increase. Tasker's panic and terror are obvious. The sound of crackling also increases.*)

Emma Farmer

Tasker: It's true.   Peter Farrell

Terry: Listen. Listen.   Daniel Garrett

Tasker: I'm getting out.   Daisy Hammond
        Where am I?

   (*He stumbles and falls.*)   Phillip Ince

                                                           Madeline Ingoldsby

Tasker: I can't see . . . I can't see . . . Daniel Kennedy

                                                           Robert Lund

                                                           Annie Price

                                                           Avril Summers

(*The names and the crackling reach maximum pitch and fade away. Silence. Then slippered footsteps.*)

Gran: Terry. Terry.

Terry: Mmh?

Gran: Terry. It's nearly eleven.

Terry: Eleven?

Gran: Time you were up. Your mother's expecting you. I couldn't let you sleep any longer.

Terry: (*Yawns.*)

Gran: Anyone would think you'd been up all night. You been out on the tiles?

Terry: What?

Gran: I was only joking. Come on, you can make us a nice cup of tea.

Terry: Gran. About those messages. I'm sorry.

Gran: Don't worry.

Terry: I couldn't help it.

Gran: I know love. I know.

Terry: I was having some trouble.

Gran: Anita told me. I understand.

Terry: Anita? She told you?

Gran: The other day when she first came. A boy, wasn't it?

Terry: Yes.

Gran: She said his name. What was it? I remember, it was Tasker. Is that right?

Terry: Tasker, that's right.

Gran: Is it all right now?

Terry: Yes, it's all right now.

Gran: That's right. These things sort themselves out. So you're not to worry about the money.

Terry: Thanks Gran. But I'll pay you back.

Gran: Just as you like. Did your teacher like the recording?

Terry: Yes they liked it, they all liked it.

Gran: Useful, was it? I like to be useful.

Terry: It was useful, all right.

Gran: I'll tell Frank everything's all right. I'll tell him tonight. He'll be pleased. I told him about the five pounds. He was cross. He never liked to see money wasted. I told him it wouldn't be wasted. You hadn't stolen it. He said you were a good boy.

Terry: Gran, when you talk to him, like, talk to Grandad, do you, can you see him?

Gran: No. It's just talking. Like on the telephone. Oh.

Terry: What is it?

Gran: Reminds me. I meant to tell you. Anita . . .

(*The phone rings.*)

Gran: She rang last night. You must have been asleep.

Terry: I'll answer it.

Gran: I couldn't wake you.

(*We hear Terry picking up the phone.*)

Terry: Hello.

Anita: Terry?

Terry: Yes. Anita?

Anita: Yes it's me.

Terry: You O.K?

Anita: Yes. You?

Terry: Tired. Just got up.

Anita: Did you go?

Terry: Course.

Anita: Terry.

Terry: You didn't know the ending, did you? I went out after him. Should have seen him run. They was all there. Duckett, Bron. They all saw how scared he was. He didn't seem to be able to see.

Anita: Terry, listen . . .

Terry: You were brilliant. I could tell he was scared even before he got there. I could tell.

Anita: Terry, I'm sorry . . .

Terry: Then you switched on the voices.

Anita: Listen.

Terry: I almost believed it myself.

Anita: Terry, listen. Listen. That's what I wanted to tell you. I couldn't get out.

Terry: Couldn't?

Anita: I couldn't do it. I'm sorry. I tried to ring you. I couldn't face it. I went back to bed. I'm sorry.
Terry?
Are you there?
Terry?
Terry.

(*Chord of music. Crackling. The names are repeated, gradually fading.*)

Activities

A play is usually written to be performed rather than just read. *Voices* is a radio play, written to be spoken and tape-recorded, rather than presented on a stage or filmed. If you are going to put on a performance of a play, you need to study the play in order to decide exactly what the author is saying in the play and what the issues are that it explores. You need to think about the characters — what sort of person each one is, why she or he behaves in that way and what each of the characters is thinking and feeling at each point in the play. Before you go on to make a recording of *Voices*, first work through these exercises.

Thinking about the characters

Terry

1 What sort of a boy is Terry? Choose two or three words to describe his character.

2 Talk about the way Terry behaves.
  a) Why doesn't he stand up to Tasker at first?
  b) At what point does he decide to stand up to Tasker? Why does he change his mind?
  c) Has Terry changed in any way by the end of the play? If so, how and why has he changed?

3 Talk about Terry's relationship with his gran. What does the way Terry treats his gran tell you about Terry's character?

4 Compare Terry with Anita. Which of them do you think has the stronger character? Give reasons for your answer.

5 In pairs, role-play an interview with Terry. Before you begin, make a list of questions to ask him. Skim through the play and think of questions that ask him to explain why he behaved as he did and what his thoughts and feelings were at key points in the play. Here are two such questions: Why didn't you tell Miss Diamond that Tasker was bullying you? How did you feel when Miss Diamond was questioning you?

6 If you are going to play the part of Terry, you must try to get inside him, to get under his skin and understand exactly what makes him tick. One way of doing this is to imagine what Terry is like in other situations, not just those that are presented in the play. For example, what is his home like? How many people are there in his family? What are his hobbies and interests? How good at his schoolwork is he? Think about Terry in this way, then write a thumbnail sketch of him. Compare your idea of him with other people's.

Tasker, Duckett and Bron

1 What sort of things, besides bullying Terry, do you think Tasker, Duckett and Bron do together? In groups of three, role-play a scene when Tasker, Duckett and Bron are out together.

2 Talk about the relationship between Tasker and his two mates as it is shown in the play and as you showed it in your role-play. Do you think the relationship between the three of them will be altered in any way because Duckett and Bron saw how scared Tasker was at the end of the play?

3 As you read the script, what pictures did you form of Tasker, Duckett and Bron? Draw pictures of them and write a brief description of how you pictured them.

Anita

1 What is your impression of Anita? Is she the sort of person you would like to have as a cousin? Say why.

2 At the end of the play, what is Anita thinking and feeling? Either role-play a scene, or write a letter, in which Anita tells one of her friends about the plan she and Terry made, about why she did not go, and about what Terry told her happened.

Gran

1 How would you describe Terry's gran: sad and lonely? kindly and understanding? eccentric and rather frightening? sharp and thoughtful? cheerful and energetic? Talk about Terry's gran and how she behaves towards Terry, then choose two or three words to sum up your view of her.

2 Work in pairs. One of you has been given the part of Gran in a production of *Voices*, the other is her friend. Go through the script, looking at the scenes in which Gran appears. Discuss what Gran says in each scene and talk about what impression of Gran you want to try to give the audience by the way you read the part.

Miss Diamond, Miss Townsend and Mr Heard

1 What impression do you get of Miss Diamond from a) the way she talks in assembly, b) the way she interviews Terry and Tasker?

2 Work in pairs. Role-play scenes in which Miss Diamond deals with a girl or boy a) who has been caught cheating in a test, b) who is very upset because she/he has forgotten to bring her/his PE kit to school. Repeat the exercise, taking it in turns to be Miss Diamond. Afterwards, discuss how you showed Miss Diamond treating the children and talk about what sort of headteacher you think she is.

3 What sort of teachers do a) Miss Townsend, b) Mr Heard seem to be from their brief appearances in the play? If you had to choose, which class do you think you would prefer to be in — Miss Townsend's or Mr Heard's? Say why.

Thinking about the situations

Role-play the following scenes. After each scene, talk about how you showed the people behaving and say why you think they would behave in that way.

Further developments

1 What happens next? Work in pairs. Role-play either a scene in which Terry and Anita meet and Anita gets Terry to tell her exactly what happened when he and Tasker went to the school, or a scene in which Gran, who senses that something has been going on, gets Terry to tell her what it is.

2 Imagine that when Terry and Anita listen to Gran's story on the tape, they find that there is something else recorded on the tape. It is the voices of some of the children who died in the fire telling the story of what they were doing when the fire broke out. Work in a group. Produce a short script or a tape-recording telling the story of the fire.

Parallel situations

1 'You've got to stand up for yourself!' Work in pairs. A boy like Terry is being bullied. A girl like Anita tells him he's got to stand up for himself against the bullies.

2 Two children, who are doing a project on life 75 years ago, interview an old person about her memories. During the course of the interview she tells them a ghost story, just as Gran did when Anita interviewed her.

3 'You keep your mouth shut — or else!' A bully, like Tasker, threatens a smaller boy, like Terry, not to tell on him — or else!

Presenting the play

Work in groups and make a tape-recording of the play. Before you actually make the recording, hold several rehearsals in which you read the play through and practise how you are going to speak the lines. While the rehearsals are going on, the person in charge of the sound effects can be recording the necessary sounds. Here is some advice from the author, Gareth Owen: 'In recording, try to make the sound effects sound as natural as possible. For example, record people's footsteps as they walk perfectly naturally. The most common mistake is for sound effects to be overdone and to be too loud and intrusive.'

The sexes of the various characters may be changed and appropriate alterations made in the dialogue where the constitution of the school makes this inevitable. So, for example: Anita can become a boy or Terry a girl. The same can be done for Miss Diamond or Mr Heard.

Writing your own scripts

1 Look again at the first scene of the play. Notice how the conversation between Terry and the bullies consists of exactly the sort of things boys might say in such a situation. If you are going to write a script of a similar scene, you must make the dialogue as realistic as possible. One way of doing this is to role-play a scene and to tape-record what the characters say, then to use the recording as the basis for a script. In pairs, use this technique to produce the script of a scene in which one girl or boy is threatening another for some reason. When you are listening to the recording and preparing your script, don't just copy out what you said in the role-play. Adapt it and redraft it as you would a rough piece of writing.

2 Since this is a radio play, the scene-changes are made by using music and sound effects rather than by scenery and lighting effects as they would be in a stage play. Look at the places where the scene changes happen and talk about the sound effects which are used. Notice how the remarks which the characters make immediately after a scene change often help the audience to realise where the new scene is taking place.

Now, try to write a radio play of your own in which you use music and sound effects to make the changes of scene. Either choose a subject of your own suggested to you by the play *Voices*, or write about a group who are doing a local history project in the course of which they make a startling discovery. For example, they could discover a message which mysteriously appears on a tape-recording which one of them makes as part of the project.

2: How green you are!

BERLIE DOHERTY

The characters

BEE

JULIE

KEVIN

MARIE

ANDREW

BARBIE

MUM

MR MURPHY

Bee: There was a kid in our street called Julie. Julie Mills. None of the others could stand her. She went to a different school from us, a convent school, where they had to wear uniform. I can remember the first day she went to that school. We all watched her when she came out of the house. She was wearing a green school coat that was too big for her, and she had a stupid green hat stuck on her head, and she had her hair done up in pigtails, with green ribbons. She went bright red when she saw us.

Marie: Look at Julie Mills! What's she wearing!

Kevin: Hey, she looks like a spring cabbage.

Bee: Shut up, Kevin. She'll hear you.

Andrew: What's that she's carrying? A walking stick! Poor old lady. Shall I help you to cross the road?

Julie: Give it back. It's my hockey-stick.

Kevin: Jolly hockey sticks, old girl! Jolly ripping sport, hey what!

Bee: Ah, don't, Kevin. Leave her alone.

Andrew: Little girl's going to cry, is she? Has her mummy shut the door in her face? Has she got to go to school all on her ownio?

Marie: What's in your bag, Julie? Hey, look at her bag! It's got roses embroidered on it! Roses! And look what she's got in it! Shoes!

Bee: Julie, your bus is coming!

Andrew: Run, rabbit! Run!

Kevin (*To the tune of 'Auld, Lang Syne'*): How green you are, how green you are, how green you are, how green,

Kevin, Marie,   How green you are, how green you are, how
  green . . .

and Andrew: How green you are, how green you are, how
  green you are, how green!

Marie: That's her gone, the snob! Will you be my best friend
  now, Bee?

Bee: And I had to say yes, because I didn't want to be called a
  snob too. But I felt a bit bad about all that. Julie had been
  sort of my best friend, up till then. We used to play marbles
  together in the alleyway, and sail paper boats down the
  gutter when it rained, and all that summer we'd played
  rounders together on the beach, and helped old donkey-man
  Mooney with the donkey-rides. It felt as if none of that had
  ever happened, just because we'd started going to different
  schools. I was dying to know what hers was like, a convent
  school, with nuns like great black crows scooping her up and
  carrying her off down the corridor to chapel. I bought a bar
  of Cadbury's on the way home from school, and I went to
  her house after tea, when none of the other kids were
  around. She was still wearing that funny stiff long uniform
  when she answered the door.
  Hello, Julie.

Julie: Oh. Hi, Bee.

Bee: What was school like?

Julie: All right.

Bee: Look. I've brought us some chocolate. Cadbury's. D'you
  want some?

Julie: All right.

Bee: I thought we could sit round on the back step and share it out. Like we always do.

Julie: I can't possibly play out tonight. I've got Latin homework to do.

Bee: That did it. I went straight round to Marie Wood's house.
   Marie, can you play out?

Marie: I'm just going to have my pudding. Shall I come out after?

Bee: No, now. It's got to be now. I'll give you half of this bar of Cadbury's if you'll come and play ball against Julie's house.
   Julie was watching us from her front room, but I didn't care. We made as much noise as we could without actually breaking her window. Marie wasn't nearly as good as Julie though. She was a rotten catch. I was quite glad when her mum called her in to finish off her rhubarb crumble. But I played with Marie every night after school that week. My mum couldn't understand what was happening.

Mum: Where's Julie tonight, Bee?

Bee: Who?

Mum: You heard. Why aren't you playing with Julie?

Bee: I prefer Marie.

Mum: Marie Wood! You always said you couldn't stand her.

Bee: I can't. But she's much nicer than Julie.

Mum: I thought you and Julie were best friends.

Bee: She's a snob. She is, Mum. You should have seen her tonight, off to dancing class, swinging her new red tap shoes, showing off. She walked right past me and never even said hello. She looked at me as if I was something nasty on the pavement that you have to walk round. Something very smelly. I hate her now.

I did. And I didn't see her again for ages. I stopped even thinking about her, to tell you the truth. But then one night Marie Wood saw her on the other side of the main road; the posh part, where all the big houses are. She couldn't wait to tell me what had happened.

Marie: Hey, Bee. Guess what. I saw Julie Mills tonight.

Bee: What a treat for you.

Marie: No, listen. Guess where she was. In the posh part! I was coming up from the prom on my bike, and I saw her getting out of someone's car. It was full of snobby little girls from her convent school, and she was talking to them all posh: 'Thenk you ever so much for the lift,' she said, all plummy. 'It was so kind of you. Deddy couldn't bring the car tonight,' she said.

Bee: Deddy couldn't bring the car! Her dad's got a three-gear bike with straight handlebars!

Marie: And then, guess what! Instead of running over the main road to our street, guess what she did! She waved to them and walked backwards down the drive of one of those big posh houses.

Bee: What did she do that for?

Marie: Obvious! She's ashamed of us, that's what she is. She was pretending to those posho's that she lived in one of those big houses!

Bee: Next day Kevin and Marie and I went out to play in the alleyway after we'd been watching a cowboy film on telly. All the little kids were out too, firing caps off at cats and down letter-boxes.

Marie: Let's do that cowboy film! Those little kids can be in your wagon train, Kevin, and this lot can be Indians. I'll have this lot. I'm the Big Chief.

Andrew: You can't be the Big Chief. You're a girl.

Marie: So what? I've got the loudest voice, haven't I? I'm the one with the best ideas. I'm the one who gets things done round this place. I've got to be the Big Chief.

Julie: Hello, Marie. Hello, Bee.

Marie: Ignore her. I'm the boss round here. I'm the Big Chief.

Julie: Hello, Kevin. Hello, Andrew.

Kevin: Did someone speak?

Andrew: No, I don't think so. I can't see anyone.

Julie: Can I play?

Bee: All the kids were watching me. I broke my last stick of bubble-gum in half and shared it with Marie Wood.

Julie: Can I play, please?

Kevin: Hey, Julie. I bet you'd like to be the Indian Princess, wouldn't you?

Julie: Oh yes. Please!

Marie: Kevin Proctor, that's the star part, next to Big Chief. That's Bee's part.

Kevin: Bee doesn't mind, do you, Bee? Pretend Julie's Little Laughing Water. Pretend she's betrayed her tribe. Pretend she's got to be tied to the totem pole . . .

Julie: Oh, can I? Can I?

Marie: Kevin!

Kevin: What can we tie her with, Bee?

Bee: Marie stood staring at him, popping her bubble gum in disgust, but I suddenly cottoned on to what he was up to. Julie had betrayed her tribe.

I know, Kev! We can use our short washing-line, the one my mum uses for teatowels and dish-cloths. I'll go and fetch it.

Kevin: Come, Little Laughing Water. You are no longer a member of this tribe. What do you have to say for yourself?

Julie: Shall I start now? Oh, my dear people, this is the country that I love! These are the people of my heart! Never, never will I be untrue to my people again. What do I say next?

Marie: I vow eternal loyalty . . .

Bee: Here's the washing-line, Kev.

Kevin: Right. Tie her to the lamp-post with it.

Julie: I vow eternal loyalty . . .

Marie: To the tribe of Big Chief Sitting Bull. That's me.

Andrew: No, it's not. It's me.

Kevin: Tie it as tight as you can.

Julie: You can't both be Big Chief Sitting Bull.

Marie: Never mind. Just make your vow.

Kevin: Wind it right round her.

Julie: That hurts.

Marie: Go on . . .

Julie: To the tribe of Big Chief Sitting Bull.

Andrew: And Big Chief Running Buffalo . . .

Julie: That's stupid. You can't have two chiefs.

Kevin: Have you fastened it?

Julie: Ow.

Andrew: Say it. Go on.

Julie: And Big Chief Running Buffalo . . . . I'm starting violin lessons at school next week. The music nun says I've got wonderful pitch. She says I'm a natural musician.

Kevin: Come on, everyone. Indian file.

Julie: Hey. What's happening? Where are you going?

Kevin: How green you are, how green you are, how green you are, how green . . .

Julie: Come back! Don't leave me here!

Kevin, Marie, and Andrew: How green you are, how green you are, how green . . .

Julie: Shame! You're not going to leave me here are you?

Kevin, Marie, and Andrew: How green you are, how green you are, how green . . . How green you are, how green you are, how green you are, how green.

Julie: Help!

Bee: We went up to the top of the street in a long Indian file, and when our mums called us in to tea we all ran in and forgot about her.

    A couple of days after that I saw Julie's big sister Barbie. I was in Mrs Marriot's buying a toffee apple. Mrs Marriot's toffee apples were famous because they always had bits of cat fur stuck to them. They smelt of fish sometimes, too. I think she used to boil the toffee in the pan that she used to boil the cats' fish in. They were big, though.

Barbie: Come on, Bee Horton, are you buying or not? I'm waiting to be served too, you know.

Bee: Oh. Barbie. Hello.

Barbie: Bee, what's up with you and our Julie?

Bee: I don't know what you mean.

Barbie: Course you know what I mean. You used to go everywhere together. Why don't you go round with her any more?

Bee: I couldn't answer her. I felt really guilty. As if it was all my fault.

Barbie: We miss you at our house you know, Bee. Remember when we went to the pantomime, hey? That was fun, wasn't it?

Bee: It was all right.

Barbie: And you and Julie saved up all those sweets for me in a big tin. I'll never forget that, opening up the tin in the theatre and taking out this big sticky lump of polo mints and liquorice torpedoes and . . .

Bee: Fruit gums . . .

Barbie: Yes. And acid drops. All stuck together with bits of hair and silver paper and bus tickets sticking out of them. Remember?

Bee: And you didn't want them . . .

Barbie: It wasn't that I didn't want them! I couldn't bite anything off them! I passed it back to you and Julie and the pair of you spent the whole pantomime trying to grind bits off it . . .

Bee: We got fed up with it in the end and chucked it on the floor . . .

Barbie: And when we were going out a little lad crawled under your seat and picked it up!

Bee: It was great, that pantomime.

Barbie: Course it was, Bee.

Bee: Suddenly I couldn't talk to Barbie any more. I ran out of Mrs Marriot's. I could feel my face burning. I wish I had a big sister like Barbie.

Next day at school Kevin grabbed hold of me as I was coming out of the girls' cloakrooms. He was bursting with news.

Kevin: Bee! Have you heard?

Bee: What?

Kevin: You haven't heard!

Bee: Haven't heard what?

Kevin: About Julie Mills.

Bee: Yes. Course I have.

Kevin: Oh. Right.

Bee: Kev! Wait!

Kevin: What?

Bee: Go on. Tell me.

Kevin: I thought you knew.

Bee: Tell me!

Kevin: About Julie's accident?

Mr Murphy: Come on, Kevin Proctor. Your form's in assembly already.

Kevin: Sorry, sir.

Bee: Wait! Kevin! Wait!

Mr Murphy: And you too, young lady. Have you registered yet?

Bee: Please, Mr Murphy! Can I just ask . . . Kevin! Wait!

Kevin: He'll do us!

Bee: What happened to Julie?

Kevin: She got knocked down.

Mr Murphy: I'm counting, Proctor.

Kevin: Outside her school. She was running away . . .

Mr Murphy: Three . . .

Bee: I don't believe you, Kevin.

Mr Murphy: Two . . .

Kevin: Cross me heart and hope to die.

Bee: When? How?

Kevin: She was taken to . . . .

Mr Murphy: NOW!

Kevin: Sorry, sir. Hospital.

Bee: Hospital. Kids were surging round us down the corridor, and Kevin was carried off with them as if the tide was going out. I felt cold with dread, as if a grey hand was wiping itself across my face. Julie! I kept seeing her, lying in the road in her uniform, and being lifted up by one of the nuns, and her head lolling back. I imagined that I was there with her, and that I wanted to say sorry, and that her eyes were blank and staring right through me.

Mr Murphy: Bee Horton. Where are you supposed to be?

Bee: Sorry, sir.

Mr Murphy: Assembly. Get there. NOW!

Bee: I kept thinking about her all morning. I kept seeing her running out of school and racing across the road and slamming into a car. And lying there. Perhaps she was dead! Oh. No.

Mr Murphy: Will you get on with your work, young lady!

Bee: I didn't even know. I had to find out what had happened to her. As soon as dinner bell went I dashed out of class.

Marie: Bee! Wait! Where you going?

Bee: Home!

Marie: Ah! You can't! That's not allowed, Bee Horton.

Bee: Here. Have my sandwiches. I don't want them!

Marie: Great! All of them! Thanks, Bee!

Bee: I didn't stop running till I reached Julie's house. I was shaking. My arms and legs felt like lead weights, the way you do when you've just climbed out of the baths and all the water's draining off you. I didn't know what I was going to say to Julie's mum. I could hear her fumbling to open the door.

Julie: Hi, Bee.

Bee: Julie!
It was Julie. Pale and with her face all swollen and her arm in a sling.
Julie!

Julie: Hi.

Bee: I started laughing. I think she thought I was crying at first. I think I might have been.

Julie: Don't, Bee.

Bee: You look as if you've been to the dentist!

Julie: Don't make me laugh! Please! Oooh! It hurts!

Bee: I'm not! I'm not laughing.

Julie: Ooh! My stitches!

Barbie: What are you two laughing at? I could hear you up at the chip shop! Come on in, Bee. You put the kettle on, you know where it is. I'll get some forks and we'll sit round the fire and share this dinner out, shall we?

Bee: Honestly, that's the best fish and chips I've ever had. I felt a bit shy, going to school after. I stood on the doorstep,

grinning at poor old Julie all wrapped up like a parcel.
You know what, Julie. Your green uniform suits you.

Julie: Thanks, Bee.

Bee: And she grinned back at me, with her face all lop-sided.
I think she believed me.

Activities

How Green You Are! could be performed either as a radio play
or on stage. Before you put on a performance of the play, first
work through these exercises.

Thinking about the characters

Bee

1 a) Talk about the way Bee behaves towards Julie in the first
scene.

b) What happens later that evening that makes Bee decide
to side with the others and stop being friends with Julie?

2 a) Is there any evidence that Bee feels uneasy about or
ashamed of the way she treats Julie?

b) What do you think of her behaviour towards Julie? Do
you think she does anything she should feel ashamed of doing?

3 What is your final impression of Bee? If she was a pupil at
your school, do you think she would be popular? Say why.

Julie

1 Do you feel sorry for Julie? Does she do anything to

provoke the others by the way she behaves or is she picked on unfairly? Quote evidence from the play to support your views.

2 What would it be like to have been Julie? How do you think she felt while the others were teasing her? The events of the play are presented very much from Bee's point of view, because Berlie Doherty has chosen to make Bee the narrator. What would Julie have said if she had been the narrator? Rewrite the narrator's parts for the first two scenes and for the cowboys and indians scene with Julie as the narrator rather than Bee. When you have finished, form groups and show each other what you have written. Decide whose script most successfully captures Julie's thoughts and feelings.

3 Imagine that during her first few weeks at her new school Julie kept a diary. Write some of the diary entries that she made during those weeks.

Kevin, Marie and Andrew

1 Talk about the way Kevin, Marie and Andrew treat Julie. Are they cruel to her? Why don't they like her?

2 How do you think they will react when they learn that Bee has been to see Julie and that she has 'made it up' with Julie? In fours, role-play a scene in which they meet Bee after she has been to see Julie and ask her: 'You're not going to start going round with *her* again, are you?'

Barbie and Bee's mum

1 Bee says: 'I wish I had a big sister like Barbie.' Why? How old do you think Barbie is? What sort of a big sister do you think she is?

2 Talk about Bee's mum. Does she seem to be bossy and interfering? kindly and sympathetic? indifferent? Give your reasons.

Thinking about the situations

Role play the following scenes. After each scene, talk about how you showed the people behaving and say why you think they would behave in that way.

Further developments

1 What would have happened if Bee had an elder sister who had heard about the cowboys and indians incident? Imagine that Bee's elder sister speaks to her and suggests that Bee and her friends are treating Julie rather unfairly and cruelly. Role play a scene in which Bee's elder sister talks to her about how she is treating Julie.

2 Imagine that instead of Julie having an accident, Bee found her one day, sitting in the rec, crying bitterly. Role play what they said to each other when Bee went up to Julie and asked: 'What's wrong?'

Parallel situations

1 A group of children taunt and tease someone who dresses differently or behaves differently from them, in the way that Bee and the others tease Julie about her uniform and going to a different school.

2 A scene in which a group of children allow someone who is usually excluded from their games to join in for once, then play a trick on her, just as Bee and the others let Julie join in their game of cowboys and indians and agree to her being the Indian princess so that they can tie her up.

3 'Isn't it awful?' Two children tell each other what they have heard about an accident that has happened to someone they have been teasing, ignoring or picking on.

4 'Where have you been lately?' Work in pairs. One of you meets the older sister or brother of a person who used to be your best friend. The sister or brother asks why you don't go round together any more and you either make excuses or talk about the things you used to do together, in the way that Barbie talks to Bee.

5 a) A scene in which two children who have been best friends break their friendship because one accuses the other of being a snob.

b) A scene in which the same two friends patch up their quarrel and agree to be friends again.

Presenting the play

Work in groups of five or six. Put on a performance of the play either by tape-recording it or by giving a reading of it to the rest of the class. Because there are eight characters, some of the parts will have to be doubled up. For example, the parts of Barbie and Mum can be doubled up, so too can those of Andrew and Mr Murphy.

Writing your own scripts

1 a) Notice how in this script Berlie Doherty uses the main character, Bee, to act as a narrator. Look at the beginning and the end of each scene and talk about how she uses Bee's speeches as narrator to lead on from the previous scene and to lead into the next one. Work in pairs and draw a flow chart which shows the structure of the play and how the narrator is used to link the scenes together.

b) Work in pairs and write a script of your own about a group of children and how they treat someone who is different from them in some way, perhaps because, like Julie, they go to a different school or maybe because they speak differently or are new to the neighbourhood. Use a narrator to link together the different scenes in your play. You may find it useful, as you are working out the plot, to draw a flow chart showing the different scenes that you plan to include.

2 The author, Berlie Doherty, adapted this short play from a scene in her novel *How Green You Are!* See if you can find a copy of the novel and compare how the scene is presented in the novel with how it is presented as a playscript. Choose a scene from a novel you have read recently which you could adapt into a playscript. Use the main character to act as a narrator in the way that Berlie Doherty uses Bee in *How Green You Are!*

3: Finders keepers

DAVID WILLIAMS

The characters

DAWN SLATER, a 14-year-old schoolgirl
TRACY MOORE, a classmate
GARY BENSON, Dawn's boyfriend
MRS WADE, her form teacher
MISS FOX, her Games teacher

(In a modern comprehensive school. A classroom door opens. Corridor acoustic.)

Mrs Wade: All right, Christine. Join the other end of the line and wait there. Who's next?

Dawn: *(To herself.)* God, it's me.

Mrs Wade: Dawn Slater. Come in, please.

Dawn: *(To herself.)* I'm bright red, I can feel it. She'll know.

(Door closes.)

Mrs Wade: Sit down there, the chair beside my desk. Now, then. *(A movement of chairs.)*

Dawn: *(To herself.)* She's that close, she'll see it. Bound to.

Mrs Wade: I don't like doing this. Acting as . . . Are you listening?

Dawn: Yeah, course.

Mrs Wade: Well, lift your head up and look at me. I don't like acting as interrogator . . . but these things have to be sorted out. It's not the first time something's gone missing from this class. Is it?

Dawn: No, Miss.

Mrs Wade: So I'm determined to get to the bottom of it. I'm going to ask you the same question I've asked the others. Do you know anything about Tracy's gold chain?

Dawn: *(To herself.)* Is it showing?

Mrs Wade: Well?

Dawn: No.

Mrs Wade: Miss Fox said . . . Don't think I'm accusing you, because I'm not. The thing is, Tracy definitely had the chain on before Games this morning. Then afterwards everybody had a shower. Miss Fox tells me you were . . . lingering. Last in the shower, last out. Why?

Dawn: Dunno. No reason.

Mrs Wade: There must be a reason. Everything has a reason.

Dawn: (*To herself.*) You wouldn't get it. You know nowt about me. Foxy neither. You know nowt . . . (*Fade in shower noise.*)

Dawn: (*To herself.*) Come on, come on you lot. This rotten shower's running cold. Get out, will ya? Move it.

Miss Fox: (*Out in the changing room.*) Move along, you girls. Don't dally round here. You've . . . Who's left that shower running? Which was the last girl . . . Oh, who's that, Dawn Slater?

Dawn: Miss.

Miss Fox: Why are you still in there? You should be dressed and ready to go by now.

Dawn: I was late.

Miss Fox: Late?

Dawn: Getting in.

Tracy: She's been there ages, Miss Fox.

Dawn: Nobody asked you, big gob.

Tracy: Charming!

Dawn: Nowt to do wi' you.

Miss Fox: That's enough.

Tracy: I was just saying . . .

Miss Fox: All right, Tracy. Out you go.

Tracy: Yes, Miss Fox.

Miss Fox: And you . . . (*Turning the shower off.*) I want you dressed and out of here in three minutes flat.

(*The bell rings.*)

Make that two minutes. Are you on first lunch?

Dawn: I don't bother wi' lunch.

Miss Fox: Stupid girl. Well, I'm not going to miss mine for you. Straight out in the yard when you've done. Two minutes, no more. (*Walking away.*) Or there'll be trouble.

(*The swing door slams.*)

Dawn: (*To herself.*) So what else is new? (*Sighing.*) Least they're all away now. Wan't gonna put this blouse back on while Tracy Moore an' them were hanging about. (*Mimicking.*) 'Ooh, look at her. Fancy going round with a great hole in the elbow. Wouldn't be seen dead . . .'. (*Snorting.*) They make me sick. What do they know? La-di-da South Beach Snobby Estate. Wouldn't be seen dead . . . (*Pause.*) She could've bought us some new stuff. What's child benefit for? Me, not her. Not that I'd spend it on school uniform, like. Summat for the weekend maybe, going out wi' Gary. God, I better hurry. He'll be waiting.

Mrs Wade: (*Breaking into Dawn's thoughts.*) I'm waiting.

Dawn: Mmm? What?

Mrs Wade: You still haven't told me why you were loitering in the changing room.

Dawn: Wasn't loitering.

Mrs Wade: What time did you leave?

Dawn: Dunno. Haven't got a watch.

Mrs Wade: Are you trying to be obstructive?

Dawn: No, I'm just telling ya.

Mrs Wade: Where did you go when you were changed?

Dawn: Round by the bike sheds.

Mrs Wade: For a smoke?

Dawn: Don't smoke.

Mrs Wade: So why go to such an out-of-the-way place? Was there something you wanted to do, look at perhaps, where nobody could see you?

Dawn: No, I just . . . I always go there.

Mrs Wade: Who else was round the bike sheds? Who were you with?

(*Fade in schoolyard noises and voices in the background. Exterior acoustic.*)

Dawn: Hi!

Gary: Where you been?

Dawn: Changing. We had stupid Games.

Gary: I know. Saw ya on the field. Tanner had us marking pitches.

Dawn: Thought you had Maths this morning.

Gary: Yeah, marking pitches Maths. Makes a change from stacking chairs Maths. That's what he usually has us doing. Here, got summat for ya.

Dawn: What is it?

Gary: Gold chain. Look.

Dawn: What ... You come into money or summat?

Gary: Maybe.

Dawn: This must've cost a fortune. The chain's that thick.

Gary: Like you.

Dawn: Cheeky sod. Honest though, is this for me?

Gary: Nah, it's for Mickey Knowles, I fancy him. Course it's for you.

Dawn: It's not me birthday or nothing.

Gary: Early Christmas present.

Dawn: How much did it cost?

Gary: Shouldn't ask.

Dawn: Just wondering.

Gary: Oh, I picked it up ... cheap.

Dawn: The catch is broken.

Gary: Yeah, that's how it was cheaper. Second-hand, like.

Dawn: I don't mind.

Gary: Here, look. The catch just needs bending over. There y'are. I'll put it round your neck.

Dawn: I've always wanted one o' these.

(*They kiss.*)

Thanks, Gary.

(*Interior acoustic.*)

Dawn: (*To herself.*) Yeah, thanks for nothing. You never told us it was nicked. Coulda died when she started on about it this afternoon. You've landed me right in it, Gary Benson. What am I gonna do now? Say nowt, that's all.

Mrs Wade: You've got nothing else to say, then?

Dawn: No.

Mrs Wade: Nothing to tell me?

Dawn: No.

Mrs Wade: (*Sighing.*) All right, come with me.

(*Outside in the corridor there is a low hum of voices which stops as Mrs Wade opens the classroom door.*)

Mrs Wade: Join the back of the line, Dawn. Who's next?

Tracy: I think that's everybody, Mrs Wade.

Mrs Wade: I see. And still no culprit, mmm? Nobody who has the courage to own up to . . . a mistake. A moment of temptation you're possibly regretting now, yes? (*Pause.*) No offers. It's somebody in this class, I'm sure it is. I have my suspicions . . . Look, I don't want to bring the police in if I can help it . . .

Dawn: (*To herself.*) Jesus, me mam'll kill us.

Mrs Wade: But this is a very serious offence. That chain was worth . . . Well, really that's not the point. It's the fact that we have a thief among us. A thief.

(*Pause*)

I'm going to give you one last chance. At the end of school today my classroom will be open and empty. I will be in the staffroom for half-an-hour. At the end of that time I'll walk back into this room and open the drawer in the middle of my desk. In it I expect to find one gold chain, returned by the person who took it. If I do, no more will be said about this . . . incident. If not, I'll go straight to the Head and ask him to report a theft to the police. And you all know what that will mean. The choice is yours. All right, you can go.

(*As footsteps start down the corridor, she calls after them.*)

Remember, half-an-hour only from the end of school.

(*Fade. Exterior acoustic.*)

Gary: I didn't nick it!

Dawn: It's her chain. I was bright red. If she'd looked instead o' going on an' on . . .

Gary: If you listened 'stead o'going on . . . I'm telling ya, I didn't pinch it.

Dawn: Yeah, yeah. Tracy give it you, did she?

Gary: Course not.

Dawn: You lied to me, Gary. You said you bought it second-hand.

Gary: I never, see. I said I picked it up second-hand. That's what I did. Picked it up.

Dawn: Where?

Gary: On the field. I was bringing the marker thing back an' I saw it lying on the grass.

Dawn: She must've . . .

Gary: Dropped it during Games. Yeah, but I didn't know whose it was. So I picked it up. Finders keepers.

Dawn: Why didn't you say? Why didn't you tell me?

Gary: Well, I wanted you to think I'd bought it. Wanted it to be . . . you know, special. (*Pause.*) Sorry.

Dawn: Made me feel a right . . .

Gary: I know. I've said sorry. Never thought there'd be this fuss.

Dawn: Well, there's one good thing.

Gary: What?

Dawn: Least you know whose it is now. You can give it back.

Gary: What you mean, give it back? You didn't give it back when you was asked.

Dawn: I know, but . . . I really thought you'd pinched it. I didn't want to get you into trouble. Nor me neither. But now . . .

Gary: What's the difference now?

Dawn: Well, you can explain about finding it and it'll be OK.

Gary: That's daft. In the first place she lost it, didn't she? That was her own stupid fault. So serve her right if somebody finds it and keeps it. That's fair.

Dawn: No, it's not. You're supposed to hand things in. Otherwise it's just like stealing.

Gary: Course it isn't. It's like I said before. Finders keepers. Everybody does it.

Dawn: That doesn't make it right. Specially when you know who it belongs to.

Gary: I didn't know.

Dawn: You do now.

Gary: But I can't hand it in now. They'll just reckon I've nicked it an' chickened out 'cause of all the bother.

Dawn: Just explain . . .

Gary: Get off, you can't explain nothing to this lot. If you're in the posh set maybe, but not when they've got you marked down as rabble. You're guilty before you start. You know that.

Dawn: Yeah, I know that.

Gary: Well then, let's just forget it, right? Keep the chain and stuff them.

Dawn: I can't do that, Gary. Sorry, but I just can't. Here, have it back.

Gary: I don't want it. What do I want it for? I gave it to you for . . . you know. For you. Agh, chuck it away for all I care.

Dawn: No. (*Pause.*) Listen, do you really want to do summat for me?

Gary: Yeah, course. Anything.

Dawn: Mrs Wade said if the chain was put in her drawer after school tonight everything would be OK. Nothing more said.

Gary: I'm not creeping in her classroom . . .

Dawn: You said you'd do anything for me, Gary.

Gary: I know, but . . .

Dawn: Well, then.

Gary: They'll have the room watched.

Dawn: No they won't. She promised. Half-an-hour after school, she said. I'd do it myself, but I'm too scared.

Gary: Nowt to be scared of if there's nobody around.

Dawn: I'll do it if you come as well.

Gary: I still think we should keep it.

Dawn: Please, Gary. For me.

Gary: You're . . . All right. But I reckon you're out of your skull.

Dawn: Thanks. (*She kisses him.*) Thanks, love.

(*Fade. Interior acoustic, with a slight echo.*)

Dawn: (*Whispering.*) All clear?

Gary: Yeah. (*Opening the door gently.*) You know what's daft about this?

Dawn: What?

Gary: We're acting like we're nicking summat, not putting it back.

Dawn: My heart's thumping like mad.

Gary: Which drawer is it?

Dawn: Middle one, she said.

(*The drawer opens with a creak.*)

Ssh!

Gary: It's the flamin' drawer.

Dawn: There. Just lay it on top of that box where she can see it. Right, close the drawer. Quietly.

Tracy: (*Loudly from the doorway.*) Dawn Slater! I knew it was you.

Gary: What . . . !

Dawn: Tracy!

Tracy: Knew it was. Couldn't wait to get your filthy hands on my things.

Dawn: I never . . .

Tracy: I'm going straight to tell. And if Mrs Wade won't get the police my mum says she will. Rotten thieves.

Gary: Don't you call us thieves, I'll . . .

Tracy: You'd better not touch me, I'll scream. Mrs Wade! Mrs Wade! (*Running off.*)

Gary: Come here, you!

Dawn: Leave her, Gary. It's too late . . .

Gary: Yeah, too late now. You idiot, I told you we shoulda kept it. I damn well told ya.

Dawn: What'll Mrs Wade . . . ?

Gary: She won't get to her. I'll stop that bitch first. Come back here, you little cat. (*Running after Tracy.*) I'm gonna get you!

Dawn: No, Gary, please! You're just making it worse. We can explain. The teacher won't . . . Gary! Gary! Don't . . . Gary!

(*Her calls fade as she runs off down the corridor after them.*)

Activities

Finders Keepers is a radio play. Before you present a reading of it or make a tape-recording of it, work through these exercises.

Thinking about the characters

Dawn

1 What sort of a person is Dawn? Do you think she has a strong character or a weak character? Give your reasons.

2 Do you approve or disapprove of the way Dawn behaves? What is your attitude towards her? At which point or points in the play (if any) do you feel sorry for her or sympathise with her? Give reasons for your views.

3 In pairs, role-play an interview with Dawn. Before you begin, make a list of questions to ask her. In addition to questions about the events of the play include questions about her home and family and her interests, e.g. What is your favourite TV programme? What books and magazines do you like reading?

4 Dawn experiences a mixture of feelings during the course of the play, including fear, anxiety, anger, resentment and despair. Imagine you are going to play the part of Dawn. Work with a partner. Go through the play scene by scene and talk about what Dawn is feeling at each point in the play. Draw a diagram showing what her feelings are at each point.

5 Imagine you are Dawn. Write the diary entry that you would make that evening, saying what happened at school and how you feel about it.

Gary

1 What do you think of the way Gary behaves? What is your impression of him? Is he the sort of person you would like to have as a friend? Say why.

2 'All that fuss over a stupid chain!' Role-play a scene in which Gary tells one of his mates all about finding the chain and what happened as a result.

Tracy

1 What evidence is there that Tracy and Dawn do not like each other, even before Tracy knows that Dawn has had her chain? Why do you think they do not like each another?

2 'I knew it was her.' Role-play a scene in which Tracy tells her best friend how she saw Dawn handing back her chain.

Mrs Wade and Miss Fox

1 As you read the play, what picture did you build up in your mind of Mrs Wade? How old is she? What clothes is she wearing? What subject does she teach? Make some notes of your ideas about Mrs Wade, then write a thumbnail sketch of her. Compare your idea of her with other people's ideas of her.

2 Look again at the first scene, in which Mrs Wade questions Dawn about Tracy's gold chain. If Mrs Wade were to speak some of her thoughts aloud to herself — in the way that Dawn does at several points in the scene — what would she say? Work with a partner. Rewrite this scene to include a number of comments or 'asides' in which Mrs Wade speaks her thoughts aloud.

3 What is your impression of Miss Fox? Talk about your idea of a 'typical' games teacher. Does Miss Fox strike you as a typical games teacher? Give your reasons. If you were given the part of Miss Fox, what impression of her would you try to give the audience?

Thinking about the situations

Role-play the following scenes. After each scene, talk about how you showed the people behaving and say why you think they would behave in that way.

Further developments

1 Imagine that Gary catches up with Tracy before she can get to the staffroom. He and Dawn try to explain what really happened. In threes, act out the conversation that takes place. Do they manage to persuade Tracy not to tell Mrs Wade?

2 Imagine that Tracy reaches the staffroom before they can stop her. When she tells Mrs Wade what she saw, how does Mrs Wade react? Repeat the scene showing Mrs Wade reacting in at least two different ways. Then, discuss how you think Mrs Wade would actually have reacted. Support your view of her reaction by referring to how she behaves in the play.

3 If Tracy reached Mrs Wade before Dawn and Gary could

stop her, what would they decide to do? Act out a scene in which Gary and Dawn go off round by the bike sheds to discuss what to do.

4 In threes, act out the scene later that afternoon or some time the following day when either Gary and Dawn go to see Mrs Wade or Mrs Wade asks to see them.

5 'Have you heard?' At school the next day a group of the class who have heard both Dawn's version and Tracy's version of what happened discuss whose story they believe. They talk about why Dawn didn't own up at once, saying whether or not they think she should have done and what they would have done if they had been in Dawn's situation.

Parallel situations

1 Two children are out playing somewhere when they find something valuable, such as a watch or a ring. One of them wants to keep it, arguing that it's 'finders keepers'. The other wants to hand it in.

2 'We ought to put it back.' Two friends argue about whether or not they should hand back an object which one of them has been given, because they have learned that the object has been either lost or stolen — just as Gary and Dawn argue about whether or not they should return Tracy's chain.

3 A teacher like Mrs Wade interviews a number of pupils because something valuable has gone missing. Imagine that all the pupils are under suspicion because they all had the opportunity to take it. Before you begin, work out all the details of the situation. Then, draw lots to decide which of the people taking the parts of the pupils is the one who actually took it, by putting a piece of paper marked with a cross in among a number of blank pieces of paper. To make the situation more realistic, do not reveal who it was until after the interviews have taken place.

4 'You should own up.' A girl or a boy who has done something wrong tells a friend and asks the friend for advice about what to do. The friend argues that she or he should own up, because lots of other people are under suspicion.

Presenting the play

Work in groups of five or six. Put on a performance of the play either by tape-recording it or giving a reading of it to the rest of the class. If there are six in your group, the person who does not have a part can be in charge of making the recording and producing the sound effects.

Writing your own scripts

1 In the first scene, David Williams uses the technique of getting one of the characters, in this case Dawn, to speak her thoughts aloud in a number of comments or asides. You can use this technique not only to let the audience know exactly what a character is thinking and feeling during a scene, but also, as David Williams does, to give the audience information that is essential to the plot. Work either on your own or with a partner. Develop a short script in which a parent or teacher questions a teenager and the teenager gives evasive answers. Include some asides which let the audience know what the teenager is thinking and which give the audience information about what the teenager is keeping secret from the parent or teacher and about why they want to keep it secret.

2 Work in pairs. Talk about the ideas you developed in the role-plays in the further developments section (above), then write another scene to add to the end of the play. Try to make the way the characters speak in your scene match the way David Williams makes them speak in the play. As you write, read sections of your script aloud to make sure it sounds right. If it does not sound right, ask yourselves why and redraft it.

3 Notice how in this play the events of the plot are not presented in the sequence in which they happen. Two of the events — the scene in the changing-room and the scene in which Gary gives Dawn the chain — are presented as Dawn's memories, i.e. as 'flashbacks', during Mrs Wade's interview with Dawn. We learn about other important events, e.g. how Gary found the chain in the first place, from conversations that take place later in the day.

Work with a partner and draw a chart listing the events in the order in which they actually happened, starting with the lesson when Dawn was doing games and Gary was marking pitches. Then, by means of arrows indicate at which point in the play, i.e. during which scene or conversation, you learn about each of the events.

Now, try to write a script about an incident that occurred at a school. Develop your plot so that the audience learns about the events in a different order from the order in which they actually occurred, by using flashbacks and references in conversations, in the way that David Williams does. Before you begin to draft your script, work out a plan. You may find it helpful to draw a chart showing the events in the order in which they actually happened and then to use arrows and numbers to indicate the order in which you are going to present them in your script.

4: Up school

DAVID FOXTON

The characters

IMOGEN BEAVERBROOK, the EDITOR of the School Magazine

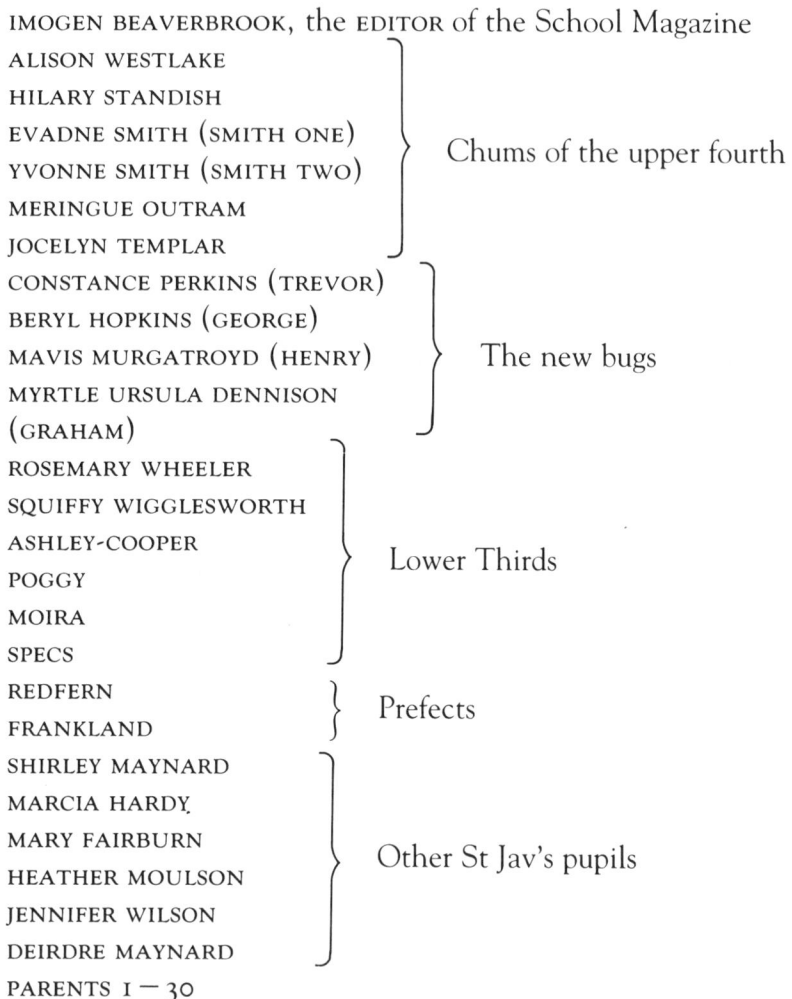

ALISON WESTLAKE
HILARY STANDISH
EVADNE SMITH (SMITH ONE)
YVONNE SMITH (SMITH TWO)
MERINGUE OUTRAM
JOCELYN TEMPLAR

Chums of the upper fourth

CONSTANCE PERKINS (TREVOR)
BERYL HOPKINS (GEORGE)
MAVIS MURGATROYD (HENRY)
MYRTLE URSULA DENNISON
(GRAHAM)

The new bugs

ROSEMARY WHEELER
SQUIFFY WIGGLESWORTH
ASHLEY-COOPER
POGGY
MOIRA
SPECS

Lower Thirds

REDFERN
FRANKLAND

Prefects

SHIRLEY MAYNARD
MARCIA HARDY
MARY FAIRBURN
HEATHER MOULSON
JENNIFER WILSON
DEIRDRE MAYNARD

Other St Jav's pupils

PARENTS 1 — 30

NEW READERS START HERE:

Editor: For all our new readers, here is the story so far. . . .
Our year began in very much the usual way here at good old
St Javelin's . . . St Jav's as we all call it . . . that merry bustle
of the first day as we renewed acquaintance with all our old
chums . . .

(*Chaos as the pupils pile on, left and right. Bell.*)

. . . soon settling down to our normal routine . . . or so we
all thought . . . dot . . . dot . . . dot . . . leave your readers
wondering, etc. . . . (*Bell*) . . . the first assembly . . .

All: Lord, behold us with thy blessing,
Once again assembled here:
Onward be our footsteps pressing,
In thy love and faith and fear:
Still protect us
By thy presence ever near.

Break temptation's fatal power,
Shielding all with guardian care,
Safe in every careless hour,
Safe from sloth and sensual snare:
Thou, our Saviour,
Still our failing strength repair.

Amen.

Editor: And then off to our dorms . . .
Garrett-Anderson (*Exit*), Nightingale (*Exit*), Fry (*Exit*)
. . . and Cleopatra (*Exit*) . . .
(*Aside*) How progressive our Founders really were . . . here at
St Jav's . . .
Meantime . . . the hoydens of the Upper Fourth were now
occupying the hallowed ground of Study 5A.

(*Enter the 'chums' — Alison, Hilary and Meringue, and pose.*)

Alison Westlake, Captain of the Second Lacrosse Team . . .

Alison: . . . Don't be feeble, you duffers, someone must know where my stick is . . .

Hilary: Is this it? . . . going shrimping again, are we, angel?

Editor: Hilary Standish . . . bit of an intelleg . . . intrellig . . . interlog . . . swot, really.

(*Fight/argument over the stick.*)

Alison: . . . Give it here this instant, Hil.

Hilary: . . . Temper, temper, don't get so ratty! (*etc.*)
(*Smith One and Two enter.*)

Smith One: . . . Steady on, you two.

Smith Two: . . . Here's the most amazing news.

Smith One: Golly! Wait till you hear.

Smith Two: . . . We have something to divulge.

Editor: The Smiths . . .

Evadne: Evadne . . .

Editor: and . . .

Yvonne: Yvonne.

Editor: (*To audience.*) No relation to each other.

Evadne:
Yvonne: } (*Hurt.*) Cousins!

Editor: (*To audience.*) Very distant.

Evadne: } Oh I say!
Yvonne: } Look here!

Editor: Ssh! How can we ever get on . . . now where were we? . . .

Hilary: Well, don't stand there like bars of soap, you horrors, tell us the news on the Rialto . . .

Meringue: On the what, Hil?

Alison: Do be quiet, Meringue, how can we ever progress? . . . Say on, troops . . .

Meringue: But I don't understand . . .

Hilary: You never do, Meringue, you gannet, let the intellectuals do the thinking.

Meringue: . . . Girls with brains ought to do something else with them besides think.

Editor: . . . One of the sayings of Meringue Outram . . . the guzzler of the Upper Fourth . . .

Meringue: . . . Anyone fancy an éclair?

Alison: Quiet, you owl . . . what's this earth-shattering news?

Evadne: You'll never guess . . .

Yvonne: Quite the most outrageous thing . . .

Evadne: What *do* you think?

Yvonne: . . . We never thought it could happen . . .

Alison: You don't mean . . .?

Evadne: That's it Ali . . . you've got it in one . . .

Yvonne: There's a new girl in the Upper Fourth.

All: Gosh!

(CONSTERNATION. *Positions adopted.*)

Editor: Not so surprising, really . . . there always were a crop of new girls . . . although 'tis true for your scribe here to record that this time the new bugs had something odd about them . . .

(*Enter the 'new bugs' . . . obviously boys in female school-dress.*)

Welcome to St Javs. I am Imogen Beaverbrook, Editor of the School Magazine and all-round good egg and I need your names for the Salvete . . . so you are? . . .

Connie: My name is (*Looks inside blazer.*) Constance Perkins and I am a new . . . girl?

Editor: Bug.

Connie: Eh?

Editor: New . . . bug . . . do get things right, my readers demand it! Next . . .

Beryl: My name is (*Looks inside hat.*) six-and-five-eighths Hopkins and I am a new bug.

Editor: (*Checking the hat.*) Beryl.

Beryl: . . . a new Beryl.

Editor: Next . . .

Mavis: My name is (*Looks in football boot.*) Mavis Murgatroyd and I am . . . er . . . I am . . . er . . . I . . .

Editor: . . . a new bug also . . . and you?

Myrtle: And I'm a new bugger too.

(*MORE CONSTERNATION.*)

I'm Myrtle Ursula Dennison (*Initials on case M.U.D.*)

Editor: How apt we all thought . . . but no doubt, they would all settle down to life here . . . at St Jav's.

(*The 'new girls' are escorted off . . . in crocodile, hand in hand with another girl each.*)
Meanwhile, in study 5A . . .)

Jocelyn: (*Entering.*) I say, study 5A . . . you'll never believe what I have to tell you . . .

Hilary: Let me think . . . er . . . there's a new bug joining us in here . . .

Jocelyn: Wow, Hil, you really must be frightfully clever.

Hilary: I am.

Alison: Don't be such an ass, Jocelyn Templar — we know already — the Smiggy's let the cat out of the proverbial bag.

Jocelyn: Yes, but it's dashed inconvenient . . . I mean there's barely room for the six of us . . .

Hilary: Seven — you're forgetting Meringue counts as two.

Yvonne: Oh Hil, what a perfectly rotten thing to say.

Evadne: Poor Meringue.

Meringue: No more sausage rolls for you at midnight feasts . . . so there. (*Puts out her tongue.*)

Hilary: Gosh, Meringue, you really to know how to hurt a chap . . .

Jocelyn: Seven in a study . . . the blessed school really is going downhill rapidly . . .

Alison: Cheer up chums, she may be wizard at 'crosse and we're looking for a sound Cover Point.

Meringue: And have masses of tuck, and a father who owns a chocolate factory.

Jocelyn: Oh Meringue – you oaf!

Evadne: Cave chums! Here she comes now . . .

Yvonne: Look out, study 5A . . . here she is with that wet fish Imogen Beaverbrook.

(*Editor and Myrtle enter through centre frame.*)

Editor: Hello, chaps!

All: Hello, Imogen . . . !

Editor: Here's a new bug for you . . . Myrtle Dennison.

Jocelyn: . . . Myrtle. What a perfectly spiffing name.

Alison: I say, what position are you best in . . . ?

Meringue: . . . Have you brought any chocs?

Evadne: } We're the Smiths . . . I'm (Evadne) and she's (Yvonne)
Yvonne: }   (Yvonne)   (Evadne).

Hilary: Quiet, you terrors . . . calm down . . . welcome, my angel one . . . to the holy of educational holies.

(*Move into study frame.*)

Editor: And so term began . . . the daily round, the common task . . . life was never a bed of roses at St Javelin's . . . and yet with this particular bunch of new bugs . . . some different

scent was in the air . . . were they up . . . to . . . something
. . . large . . . question . . . mark.

CONSPIRACY

Myrtle: Right then, fellows . . . we're in . . . and no one
suspects . . . .

Mavis: Yes, but look here, Graham . . .

Myrtle: Myrtle . . .

Mavis: Quite . . . I mean, how long has this charade to
continue . . . what?

Connie: He's right . . .

Mavis: *She's* right . . .

Connie: Sorry, Henry . . .

Mavis: . . . Mavis . . .

Connie: Quite . . . how far must we go . . .

Myrtle: Until the school is undermined . . .

Beryl: Under-whatted?

Myrtle: . . . mined . . . we're sort of . . .

Mavis: Bad eggs?

Myrtle: That's it . . . we're here to get the school a bad
name . . .

Connie: Gosh, Graham.

Mavis: Myrtle.

Connie: Sorry, Henry.

Beryl: Mavis.

Myrtle: Thanks, George.

Mavis: Beryl.

Myrtle: We get the school a bad name . . . the parents take away all their little girlies . . . and our paters can move in and purchase the premises . . . lock, stock and lacrosse pitches and turn it into another kipper factory.

Mavis: Devastating!

Connie: Spiffing!

Beryl: Tophole wheeze!!

(*They shake hands.*)

Mavis: But how?

Myrtle: How?

Connie: Yes, how?

Myrtle: . . . introduce . . . bad . . . habits.

Beryl: You mean . . . like . . . nail-biting.

Connie: . . . and staying up late.

Myrtle: Worse than that . . .

Beryl:
Connie: } Gosh!

Myrtle: Gambling.

Mavis: Super!

Myrtle: Drinking!

Mavis: ⎫
Connie: ⎭ Splendid!

Myrtle: Smoking!

Mavis: ⎫
Connie: ⎬ Golly!
Beryl: ⎭

Beryl: . . . and *girls*!

Myrtle: . . . you know, Beryl, sometimes I really don't think you fully understand.

THE DASTARDLY PLAN BEGINS

(*The Hockey Match, Lower Thirds playing:
the rest of the school supporting.*)

Crowd: Come on Javs! Hurrah! the School! Up School!

Jocelyn: What's the score, Ali?

Alison: Not now, you duffer! Can't you see I'm umpiring?

Hilary: We're losing six − nil . . .

(*Crowd all groan.*)

Sorry, seven − nil . . .

Jocelyn: Well they *are* only Third-Formers.

(*Whistle.*)

Meringue: Half-time. Anyone got any biscuits?

(*Crowd freeze: team enter in disarray and group centre.*)

Rosemary: Come on, team . . . we must do better.

Squiffy: I'm worn out, Wheeler.

Rosemary: Pull yourself together . . .

Ashley-Cooper: It's awfully hard work, Wheeler.

Poggy: . . . and they're very wough, Wheeler.

Moira: St Consumpta's always are, you goose . . .

Rosemary: It isn't a tea-party, Poggy . . .

Specs: Talking of tea, where's the oranges? I'm parched.

Moira: Here's Perkins now with the refreshments.

(*Enter Connie with a tray of brown bottles.*)

Rosemary: . . . Where's the oranges, Perkins?

Connie: . . . I thought you might prefer a change . . .

(*They are handed out.*)

Rosemary: Really, Perkins . . . just when we needed *real* refreshment (*Drinks.*) . . . although, on second thoughts . . .

All team: (*Having taken swigs.*) . . . Mmmm! GUINNESS IS GOOD FOR YOU!

(*Whistle.*)

Rosemary: Come on St Jav's!

(*They roar off.*)

Crowd: Go it, St Jav's. Go! Go! Go!

(*All exeunt.*)

Editor: Sports News.
Captained by Rosemary Wheeler, the Lower Third Team had an astounding win over our old rivals, St Consumpta's,

the final score being St Jav's 17: St Consumpta's 7. The team was truly in-spired!

(*Crowd and team cross stage, singing 'Nellie Dean'. Jubilation. Turns to Prefects' Room. Mavis knocks: in the room, Redfern and Frankland.*)

Redfern: Come!

(*Mavis Murgatroyd enters.*)

Now then. Murgatroyd, isn't it?

Mavis: Yes!

Redfern: Yes . . . Redfern!

Mavis: Yes . . . Redfern.

Frankland: It's about this . . . (*Shows packet of cigarettes.*) Well? . . . I said 'Well?' . . . You do know what these are . . . don't you?

Mavis: Er . . . No.

Frankland: No . . . Frankland.

Mavis: No . . . Frankland . . . what are they?

Redfern: They were found in *your* locker, Murgatroyd.

Frankland: Do you deny it?

Mavis: Golly, gosh no! (*Pause.*) But I've no idea what they are.

Redfern: Oh come now . . .

Frankland: Don't be such an ass . . . you must know . . .

Mavis: No . . . unless . . .

Redfern: ⎫ Yes??
Frankland: ⎭

Mavis: . . . Could they be? . . . cigarettes?

Redfern: What?

Mavis: Cigarettes!

(*Pause.*)

Frankland: And what are they for, Murgatroyd?

Mavis: I thought you'd never ask . . . look I'll show you.

Redfern: ⎫ Scrumptious. Thanks, Murgatroyd.
Frankland: ⎭ You're a sport.

(*Study 5A*)

Hilary: Myrtle, how clever you are.

Myrtle: Thanks, Hil.

Meringue: What a compliment from the brains of the Upper Fourth.

Hilary: Don't be a goose, Meringue, I mean it . . .

Yvonne: Explain it to us again.

Alison: No! No! Wait . . . let me see, if I've got it right . . . ready? . . . If I'm the Bank and I have twenty then I pay twenty-ones and pontoons.

Hilary: . . . and five-card tricks, darling . . . don't forget that . . .

Myrtle: Right first time . . . so are we ready? . . .

Evadne: I say, girls . . . what a spiffing wheeze of a game . . . and can we all play?

Meringue: Hurry up, tea's in a jiff . . . we don't want to miss all the scoff.

Myrtle: What stakes, then?

Meringue: Steaks? No . . . it's always scrambled egg on Tuesdays.

(*Freeze. Group entering stage left.*)

Shirley Maynard: I say, what've you got there?

Marcia Hardy: What does it look like?

Mary Fairburn: It's a newspaper, you duffer!

Shirley: All right . . . keep your wool on . . . I was only asking. And anyway the Head doesn't approve of our reading those terrible rags.

Heather: Pooh to the Head! How else will we find out the winners at Kempton Park?

Jennifer Wilson: And what happened to my shilling each way?

Mary: Cave, chaps, prefect coming.

Redfern: What're you lot doing here? Shouldn't you all be in prep?

All: Gosh, Redfern. Sorry, Redfern. Just going, Redfern.

(*They move to go right.*)

Redfern: Wait a minute . . . all of you . . . just stand where you are.

All: Yes Redfern . . . ? (*They turn.*)

Redfern: What came first in the three-thirty?

(*Huddle round newspaper at stage right.*)

Editor: Preparations will soon be in hand for the School
Play . . . and we all know who'll be the lucky one to play the
lead . . . aren't we all biffed on Deirdre Mayweed?

(*Enter Deirdre.*)

Mavis: Excuse me: you're Deirdre Mayweed, aren't you . . .

Deirdre: That's right. And who are you?

Mavis: I'm Mavis . . . er . . . (*Looks in blazer.*) Murgatroyd
. . . Four Alpha . . .

Deirdre: And what do you want?

Mavis: Well it's just that I wondered . . . since you're in the
school play whether you could make use of this (*Hands over
bag.*) . . . It's . . . it's . . . make-up.

Deirdre: Oh, how sweet of you . . .

(*Mavis goes rapidly.*)

What a darling child . . . now let me see what's here . . .
lipstick . . . and powder . . . and . . . gosh, I say, a note . . .
'Dearest Deirdre . . .

Myrtle: . . . We all think you are stunning . . .

Connie: . . . we are really biffed on you . . .

Mavis: . . . can we meet somewhere soon? . . .

Beryl: . . . Your most ardent admirers.

Deirdre: PS We hope you can dance.' Oh those silly little
Four Alphas. (*Exits.*)

Myrtle: . . . and now we write a letter to the Sixth Form at
King Athelstan's . . .

Beryl: . . . but they're **boys**!

Myrtle: . . . Beryl . . . there are times when I wonder if you are the right girl for the job.

(*Exeunt. Enter Ashley-Cooper furtively.*)

Frankland: Who are you and where are you going?

Ashley-Cooper: If you please, Frankland, I'm Ashley-Cooper of the Lower Third.

Frankland: And why aren't you in your dorm? You're risking several Order Marks, you know.

Ashley-Cooper: Gosh, Frankland. Sorry, Frankland . . . but we've got some cases for the sick bay . . .

Frankland: Does Matron know . . . ?

Ashley-Cooper: Thought we'd tell her later, Frankland.

Frankland: Well . . . go ahead . . . but be quick.

Ashley-Cooper: Thanks Frankland . . . you're a brick. (*Calls offstage.*) Come on . . .

(*Procession of crates of lager, Bass, Guinness, light ale, brown ale, cross stage.*)

Connie: You know what to do now?

Ashley-Cooper: All arranged, Perkins . . . one case per bedside locker . . . that's 5 multiplied by two dozen bottles . . . each retailing at 1/8d plus 4d deposit per bottle (returnable), should give us an income of . . . £12 . . .

Connie: . . . minus our overheads . . .

Ashley-Cooper: What overhead, Perkins?

Frankland: Me for one . . . Ashley-Cooper.

Ashley-Cooper: Of course, Frankland . . .

Connie: . . . and then there's Matron's cut . . .

All: Ah!

LETTERS HOME

Editor: Dearest Mummy and Daddy,
   . . . You have often said that we are better educated than
   your generation. What is really true is that we go to school
   longer — which is not the same thing . . .

Jocelyn: It is really tophole to be back at St Jav's, and I'll
   wager you never thought to hear your little girlie say that. It
   is absolutely wizard. We have a new bug in our study this
   term and she is settling down well, and teaching us all sorts
   of things. Could you please see your way to increasing my
   allowance? . . . Cash is awfully scarce . . .

Heather Moulson: . . . and Jennifer Wilson said that it was
   awfully bad form, but then the going was soft and you can't
   expect the favourite always to come through with flying
   colours as our new bug Beryl Hopkins says . . .

Ashley-Cooper: Miss Fanshawe is awfully pleased about my
   mental arithmetic . . . She says it is amazing how my
   pounds, shillings and pence have improved. Incidentally
   could you ask Daddy who his wine merchant is . . .

Deirdre Mayweed: . . . It is awfully difficult to meet new
   people, but Mavis our new bug, knows masses of people and
   she says they would be only too pleased to meet us socially
   and she feels certain we could go places together . . . she
   says . . .

Heather: . . . Perhaps you wouldn't mind if I didn't come home at half-term. Beryl has invited us to her family's place near Epsom — she must be moving soon, because she said we ought to be there for the end of the flat . . .

Ashley-Cooper: . . . Constance is a real hoot, Mummy, and tells us the most fascinating stories in the dorm after lights out. We all laugh and laugh and then she says we should take more water with it . . . and that makes us all laugh more. Squiffy Wigglesworth was sick four times last Wednesday . . .

Deirdre: . . . Still, Mavis says everyone should pay for their pleasures and so one doesn't mind cutting her in for 10%, so toodle-pip for now, Mumsie . . .

Jocelyn: . . . and we're all finding it much more interesting than good old 'crosse — even Alison says so. With love from Jocelyn. PS Don't delay sending the wherewithal.

Heather: PS Beryl is only giving evens that you'll let me go.

Ashley-Cooper: PS How much corkage do they charge at Claridges?

Deirdre: PS Isn't the tango exciting?

Editor: PS Training is everything. A cauliflour is only a cabbage with a proper education.

(*Meanwhile* . . .)

Mavis: A telegram . . .

Myrtle: To Messrs Rookham . . .

Mavis: Wreckham . . .

Connie: Chicanery . . .

Beryl: and Profit Limited . . .

Myrtle: Estate Agents . . .

Connie: Land Grabbers . . .

Beryl: And Kipper Factors . . .

Mavis: Plan goes well.

Myrtle: School going to the dogs . . .

Connie: Every Thursday night.

Beryl: Stop.

Myrtle: Bad habits abound.

Beryl: Stop.

Connie: Girls now know how to drink.

Beryl: Stop.

Mavis: Smoke.

Beryl: Stop.

Myrtle: Gamble.

Beryl: Stop.

Connie: But *don't* know how to . . .

Beryl: Stop.

Alison: The answer's no . . . a definite no!

Hilary: Oh Alison don't be a killjoy . . . it's only a little roulette wheel.

Alison: . . . yes but in the Lacrosse Pavilion of all places, Hilary.

Hilary: I know . . .

Alison: I mean . . . where will I put the *chemin de fer*?

Hilary: . . . thanks Ali.

(*Exit Hilary.*)

Alison: . . . and where will Deirdre rehearse the striptease?

(*Exit Alison.*)

Moira: I say have you done this problem . . .

Specs: Show me . . . hm . . . of course.

Moira: Let's have a look . . .

Specs: Not likely.

Moira: But it's awfully hard, don't cha know, and you're good at maths . . . it's all got to be done today . . . for 3 o'clock . . .

Specs: You weren't listening when it was explained . . .

Moira: But it's hard, Specs, fiendishly diff. . . . be a sport and help out a chum.

Specs: Well . . .

Moira: Oh do, Specs . . . go on . . .

Specs: Very well, Moira, just this once . . . now look . . . you have ten shillings . . . right?

Moira: Yes . . . I've got that (*Shows ten shilling note.*)

Specs: Well this is the Round Robin, you see — an easy 10 shilling bet . . . you pick three horses, for simplicity we call them A, B and C. Now, you have 1 shilling on A, any to come 1 shilling B and 1 shilling C, you have 1 shilling on B, any to come 1 shilling A, and 1 shilling C, and you have 1 shilling on C any to come 1 shilling A and 1 shilling B. You also have 3 times 1 shilling cross-doubles plus 1 shilling cross-treble . . . altogether 10 bets equals 10 bob . . . easy!

Moira: Oh yes . . . now I get it . . . gosh, thanks, Specs.

Specs: Don't mensh. (*Takes 10 shilling note.*)

Moira: And now what about this one (*Another note.*), where I have to perm any eight from fifty-six . . .

Specs: (*Going off.*) Oh really . . .

Moira: Specs! . . . come back . . . wait a minute . . .

Mavis: . . . Wait a minute, Deirdre . . .

Deirdre: Not now, not now, Mavis, I'm in a terrific hurry.

Mavis: But I've got a huge list of bookings for your act, Deirdre . . . What shall I do with it? . . .

Deirdre: I'm far too ladylike to tell you, Mavis.

Ashley-Cooper: You're quite sure it's safe?

Shirley: (*Nods.*)

Ashley-Cooper: An old family recipe, you say.

Shirley: (*Nods.*)

Ashley-Cooper: Certainly smells good.

Shirley: (*Nods.*)

Ashley-Cooper: What d'you say it's called?

Shirley: Moonshine!

(*Mavis, Myrtle, Connie and Beryl cross stage rubbing their hands
and congratulating each other.*
But soon . . .)

Frankland: Murgatroyd! Murgatroyd! Where are you, you
little tick?

Mavis: Coming, Frankland.

Frankland: Now listen here, you little worm — where's our
Capstan Full Strength? You promised us two hundred . . .
and poor old Redfern's absolutely gasping for the weed. . . .
So where are they?

Mavis: . . . er . . . I'm not quite sure, Frankland.

Frankland: . . . Not sure! not sure! Now listen here, you little
sprout . . . you promised us and unless you want to cool your
heels in Prefect's Detention every night you will deliver what
I believe they call the goods — do I make myself clear?

Mavis: Yes, Frankland . . . I understand, Frankland.

Myrtle: It's called blackmail.

Connie: . . . or intimidation.

Beryl: . . . or threats.

Editor: . . . or indeed just deserts, according to one's judicial
upbringing. Certainly the new bugs began to find the going
far from good . . . as they say in . . . some . . . circles:
something was undoubtedly rotten in the state of . . .

Yvonne: Any sign of your postal order yet, Dennison?

Myrtle: . . . er . . . no . . . Yvonne . . . not as yet.

Evadne: Debts should be paid on time you know — a rule of
the house.

Myrtle: Quite, I do understand.

Yvonne: Wouldn't want to get, you-know-who to lean on you, would we, Smig One?

Evadne: Hardly, Smig Two, not on an old chum.

Yvonne: Although perhaps . . . we could make an exception in your case, Dennison.

Myrtle: Grooh! Yarooh! No, let go you beasts . . . I'll pay, I'll pay.

(*Exit Myrtle, blubbing.*)

Evadne: Hate to see a new bug blubbing . . . bad for the school.

Yvonne: Good for business though?

Evadne: Quite! (*They shake hands.*)

(*Enter Meringue.*)

Meringue: Well?

Yvonne: She'll pay.

Evadne: Not to worry, Meringue, . . . you'll get your money.

Yvonne:
Evadne: } Or we'll know the reason why!

Ashley-Cooper: Production?

Shirley: Five gallons per day now, the boiler house team is working all-out. They're grand types.

Connie: Excuse me, Ashley-Cooper.

Ashley-Cooper: Sales?

Jennifer: Up ten per cent on last month and the prediction is good for next.

Connie: Excuse me, Ashley-Cooper.

Ashley-Cooper: Distribution?

Squiffy: All under control, AC. School consumption monitored and adequately covered . . . orders are flowing in . . . as much as we can produce.

Connie: Excuse me, Ashley-Cooper.

Ashley-Cooper: Accounts?

Specs: All in order, AC, . . . all books balance. Profit margin high.

Ashley-Cooper: Well done . . . our side . . . congrats, all round.

Connie: Excuse me, Ashley-Cooper.

Ashley-Cooper: What do you want?

Connie: It's about my part in all this.

Ashley-Cooper: Your part? *Your* part?

Connie: Yes . . . I thought I was in on this.

Jennifer: Not likely.

Squiffy: Some hopes.

Specs: You must be joking.

Ashley-Cooper: Explain it someone.

Squiffy: You're a new bug . . . you can't expect to be involved.

Connie: But . . .

Ashley-Cooper: No buts . . . Perkins . . . you're most definitely out.

Connie: . . . here, I say . . .

All: OUT!

Deirdre: That's the way it is, Mavis, and you must accept it.

Beryl: But, Deirdre . . . it really is most awfully unfair . . .

Deirdre: I have had a better offer, that's all . . . and that's that.

Beryl: But who, Deirdre . . . who . . . do tell . . . ?

Deirdre: One of those Sixth Formers from King Athelstan's . . . says he can manage me much better.

Beryl: Oh come off it, Deirdre!

Deirdre: It's true, Mavis, there comes a point in a girl's career when she needs handling really carefully . . .

(*Exit Deirdre. Mavis does a double-take.*)

Editor: Ah! I hear my readers comment, 'But what of the parental response? . . . what will the aged parents make of this change in their off-springs' education?'

1: . . . Glad to hear you are enjoying School at long last . . .

2: . . . enlightened establishment . . .

3: . . . creating lasting impressions . . .

4: . . . send us another bottle of that marvellous stuff . . .

5: . . . wine-tasting should feature in every school curriculum . . .

6: . . . done wonders for your father's lumbago . . .

7: . . . Deirdre is such a mature girl these days . . .

8: . . . value for money . . .

9: . . . education for realities . . .

10: . . . certainly, we'll bank the money for you . . .

11: . . . Daddy and I always call it a screwdriver . . .

12: . . . ask her if she has any more advice about the meeting at Newmarket . . .

13: . . . Epsom . . .

14: . . . Haydock . . .

15: . . . Ascot will be a little holiday for us all . . .

16: . . . by all means stay with your chums; Daddy and I won't mind staying longer in Monte . . .

17: . . . you seem so grown-up from your letters . . .

18: . . . so self-sufficient . . .

19: . . . confident . . .

20: . . . sure of yourself . . .

21: . . . wonderful education . . .

22: . . . Daddy prefers Craven A . . .

23: . . . one must be progressive . . .

24: . . . modern . . .

25: . . . forward-looking . . .

26: . . . inspired leadership . . .

27:   . . . standards of excellence . . .

28:   . . . superb . . .

29:   . . . brilliant . . .

30:   . . . marvellous . . .

All: We will recommend it to all our friends.

(*Exeunt.*)

Mavis: I say, Myrtle, something's a bit fishy.

Connie: Very smelly, Myrtle . . .

Beryl: And it's not smelling of kippers . . .

Myrtle: I know . . . we must face facts . . . our plan has backfired!

All: Gosh!

Editor: Something the matter with you types.

Myrtle: Oh it's you, Beaverbrook . . .

Mavis: Nothing's the matter, Beaverbrook.

Connie: Nothing at all . . .

Beryl: Nothing . . .

Editor: I just thought you looked a little down . . . perhaps I could help . . . Have you some guilty secret?

Mavis:
Connie: ⎫ No! Of course not!
Beryl: ⎭

Myrtle: Yes! We have . . . we have a really intriguing story for your School Magazine.

Mavis:
Connie: Myrtle, what are you saying?
Beryl:

Myrtle: Ssh! We are desperate.

Connie: . . . and that's not all we are.

Editor: What do you mean? (*To audience.*) Large question mark.

Myrtle: Can we go and talk somewhere . . . alone?

(*Exeunt. Editor returns immediately.*)

Editor: Now *you* might think that that's the end of the story . . . but more was to happen . . . on Speech Day.

(*The bulk of the School enters, rather dishevelled, carrying boards proclaiming 'St Javelin's'. They sing the School Song as they enter and set the stage for Speech Day.*)

All: (*Sing*)
Floreat St Javelin's, we're the School that always wins.
Floreat St Javelin's, free from snare and sensual sins.
We will always pull together.
Both in fair and stormy weather,
There'll be always helping hands —
While our School for ever stands.

(*A second Chorus may be sung if necessary.*)

Redfern: Quiet School! Quiet! Stand still until the Staff and Headmistress arrive . . . (*A hand up*) . . . Yes?

(*Ashley-Cooper whispers to Redfern.*) . . . Oh yes . . . School . . . you may smoke!

(*Quite a lot do so. Frankland and Poggy enter with some rope: they go and speak quietly to Redfern.*)

Redfern: Thank you, Frankland! School! Fags . . . out! I've just learned that the Headmistress, and the Staff for that matter, find themselves unavoidably tied-up at the moment. So we must carry on without them.

(*Cheers.*)

Frankland: I call upon Rosemary Wheeler to read out the prize-winners; as your name is called please come forward . . .

Rosemary: The Ladbroke Prize for Applied Mathematics — Marcia Alstead!

(*Applause and cheers as they accept their awards.*)

The Phyllis Dixey Prize for Deportment — Deirdre Mayweed!
The Woodbine Cup for Physical Education — Eileen Redfern!

(*She coughs magnificently as she accepts it!*)

The Johnny Walker Prize for Applied Chemisty — Barbara Ashley-Cooper.
The Capone Prize for Consideration to Others — Wilhelmina Outram!
The Chatterley Prize for English Literature — Imogen Beaverbrook.

(*Applause — but no Imogen.*)

Imogen Beaverbrook!

(*Still no one . . . there is concern on stage.*)

Imogen: (*Running on.*) . . . Quiet School! Listen! It's the scoop of the year, of the century. . . . Wait till you hear this . . . you'll all be astounded . . .

(*Ad lib. queries* — '*Tell us*', *etc.*)

Imogen: Quiet, then . . . listen, it's . . .

(*The School freezes and she breaks forward.*)

Imogen: (*To audience*) . . . Now, here's the problem . . . should I tell them about the new bugs or should I keep the knowledge to myself? After all, there must be something to be gained from knowing who the boys are in an all-girls school . . . of course the boys tell me they wanted to change the School, to give it a bad name . . . I wonder if they've succeeded . . . ?

(*Boards turn round and read 'St Trinian's'. The School now sings.*)

All: Floreat St Trinian's: we're the best at all the sins
Floreat St Trinian's: smoking pot and downing gins,
Cheating, swearing, betting, drinking —
And the other things you're thinking
We do really best of all
Good old Trinian's beats them all!

(*Then a fight.*)

TO BE CONTINUED.

Activities

Up School is written as a stage play, but it can also be read and tape-recorded for presentation as a radio play. Before you put on a performance of the play, first work through these exercises.

Thinking about the characters

Whether you are presenting the play on stage or just tape-recording it, the important thing to realise about the characters in *Up School* is that they are not meant to represent 'real' people in the sense that the characters do in the other plays in this book. That's because *Up School* is a light-hearted play, designed to make fun of the type of school stories told in comics and girls' school books. The aim is to entertain rather than to reflect real life, so the pupils in *Up School* are presented — as they are in girls' school stories — as caricatures rather than as fully-drawn characters.

1 a) Talk about what a caricature is: the presentation of a person in a story or play in a way which exaggerates one or two of their features to produce a comic effect. Discuss any school stories you have read recently in comics, magazines or books. Are the people in them presented as caricatures? Talk about the school series shown on TV. Are the pupils presented as 'real' people or as caricatures?

b) Now look at how the 'chums of the Upper Fourth' are presented in *Up School*. Make a list of the six girls who share Study 5A. Discuss each of them in turn and talk about which of their features — if any — are exaggerated. Which of them stand out most clearly as caricatures?

2 Talk about how, throughout the play, the reactions of the characters to the situations are exaggerated. For example, the characters respond to the arrival of some new bugs as if it is a tremendously exciting event. Find other examples of the characters reacting in an exaggerated way to something that happens in the play.

Thinking about the situations

1 Imagine you are writing the programme notes for a production of the play. You have been asked to write a summary of the plot to tell the audience what the play is going to be about. Write your summary, using not more than 150 words, then compare your account of the plot with other people's.

2 The plot of the play is developed through a series of short scenes. Work with a partner and draw a flow diagram showing the sequence of the scenes. Then, form groups of four and talk about each scene in turn. Discuss what happens in it and say whether or not you found it funny and why. Rate each scene on a three-point scale: a three-star scene — very funny; a two-star scene — quite funny; a one-star scene — not very funny. Compare your rating of scenes with other groups' ratings of them.

3 Imagine you work for a comic. You have been asked to adapt the story of *Up School* to present it as a comic-strip. Choose one or two of the scenes and present it/them as a picture-strip. You can either use the script as it stands for your speech bubbles and captions or you can add to the script and adapt it as you think necessary.

Presenting the play

1 There are a lot of short scenes in this play. Whether you are presenting it on stage or tape-recording it, you will need to think carefully about how you are going to link them together. If you are tape-recording, you could use music or other sound effects, and you could get the person playing the part of the Editor to read the linking captions such as: 'New Readers Start

Here' and 'The Dastardly Plot Begins'. If you are putting on a stage production, you could use placards to present such 'chapter headings'.

2 An important problem you must solve, if you are doing a stage production, is how to arrange any furniture on stage. There won't be time to move any furniture between scene changes, but you could set up the stage so that one part of it represents, for example, Study 5A. This needs careful thought, because there is going to be a lot of coming and going, as the scenes should follow rapidly on from one another, keeping the pace of the play moving. Appoint one or two people to work with the producer on this problem. Draw some plans of the stage, showing possible ways that the furniture could be laid out. You may have to try one or two layouts in rehearsal to see what works, before you hit on the right arrangement.

3 A word of caution. In a play like this, in which characters often speak and behave in an exaggerated way, it is easy for inexperienced actors 'to go over the top' and to over-act. If you over-act you will distract your audience. Concentrate rather on getting the timing of your speeches right. That's more important than speaking your lines in a very exaggerated 'posh' way.

Writing your own scripts

1 In *Up School* the characters speak in a very different way from the way children normally speak. That's because the author, David Foxton, is poking fun at the way writers of girls' school stories make the characters in their stories behave. So he makes his characters use outdated expressions such as 'tophole wheeze' and 'spiffing' and 'posh' phrases such as 'dashed inconvenient'.

In groups, look at three or four pages of the script and find other examples of the characters using such expressions.

Now, try it yourself. Write a scene in which the chums of the Upper Fourth hold a meeting in Study 5A, because something dramatic has just happened and they must decide 'pronto' what to do about it, 'before someone blabs'.

2 Talk about the role of the Editor in the play. Notice how the Editor is both an outsider, acting as a narrator and a commentator on the events, and one of the characters, a girl called Imogen, who also has a part to play in the plot. Discuss how David Foxton uses the Editor's comments to poke fun at the way girls' school stories are written: '. . . were they up . . . to . . . something . . . large . . . question . . . mark.' Can you find other examples?

Think about an adventure story-book which you have read, e.g. a book by Enid Blyton. Write a script poking fun at the type of adventure that the Famous Five or Secret Seven have, using an editor to set the scene and to make fun of the way such stories are written, in the way that David Foxton uses the Editor in *Up School*. Work with a partner and draft the first two scenes of such a script.

5: Whiteghosts

TONY COULT

This play was commissioned and first performed in 1984 by Theatre Centre, London, under the title *Hidden Meanings*.

Cast: Rizwan Abbasi, Trevor Gordon, Faith Tingle, Tricia Wilcock

Director: Bill Mitchell

Designer: Bill Mitchell, with Marilyn Bullen, Rob Luxton.

Musical Director: Keith Morris

I would like to thank all the cast for helping me to develop the play in rehearsal, and particularly to thank Bill Mitchell, to whom the play is dedicated. T.C.

The characters

GORDON, a Bristol teenager
DIANE, a Bristol teenager
ISSIE, an African girl of the 1780s
OLU, Issie's brother, also known as Jacob

Bristol, a port. Winter, 1780s and 1980s. A cellar in old houses by the river. The houses are due for demolition. There is rubbish on the floor and graffiti on the walls. A metal ring is set into the wall. A small barred window or ventilation brick is set just above head height. A door, with chalked drawings on. They are 'stickmen' versions of things that have happened to the characters from the 1780s. There are huts, trees, people in a circle, men with guns, a ship, a man hitting two people with a stick, etc.

Attached to the metal ring by chains are two black slaves, Issie and Jacob. They are asleep, covered in sacking. They are between 15 and 17 years old, and wear dingy, torn, European clothing. For them, it is some time in the 1780s, when Bristol was a slave port.

In the 1980s, a commotion from behind the audience. Two Bristol teenagers, Gordon and Diane, run in, breathless. [NB in the original Theatre Centre production, Gordon was played by an actor of Asian origins.]

Diane: Quick! In here!

Gordon: Ssssshhh!

Diane: I feel sick!

Gordon: Don't be sick here, they'll hear you.

Diane: Are they still there?

Gordon: Quiet a minute.

(They listen.)

Diane: Are they?

Gordon: No. I think they've gone.

Diane: What if they find us? What if they come down here?

Gordon: I don't think they will. Not if we stay quiet. Listen.

Diane: Nothing.

Gordon: We'll have to stop here for a bit.

Diane: (*Looking round the cellar.*) Urgh! What is this place?

Gordon: It smells. I bet there's rats down here.

Diane: Don't!

Gordon: We're near the river. There's bound to be rats.

Diane: I don't wanna know.

Gordon: We'd better get used to it. They might still be up there.

Diane: (*To audience.*) See, it all started when I was walking down this road. There's *this* bloke going the same way. Then suddenly, in front of us, six or seven lads. Six or seven stupid smiles on their faces, too. Like there was some joke we weren't supposed to know. They started to call him — Gordon — names. I don't know why, but it got my back up. So I started in, calling *them* names. Trouble! That's when they came for us.

Gordon: (*To audience.*) Walking down this road, minding my own business. Then there's these six or seven kids — they're always there, calling names. Well, suddenly, there's this girl — Diane — and she's calling *them* names back! I tried to stop her, but. . . (*Shrugs.*) Anyway, they didn't like it. They started coming for us.

Diane: So we looked at each other, and ran.

(*They run. As they run:*)

Diane: I'm Diane. Who are you?

Gordon: I'm Gordon. What you doing?

Diane: Bunking off.

Gordon: Me too. Look out, they're coming!

(*They stop running.*)

Gordon: Playing truant. From school. Why? I don't like it. I'm scared of school.

Diane: Me, I'm bunking off the Home. That's one of those places they put you in if you're taken into care, if you can't be good. If your parents can't manage you, that kind of thing.

Gordon: The gang kept coming.

Diane: So we kept running.

Gordon: Down to the old houses by the river. Down some steps, and into this smelly dump.

Diane: Funny how quick you can be mates with someone you've never met.

(*Gordon turns back from the audience and looks at the cellar.*)

Gordon: What is this place?

Diane: Some kind of old houses. They're knocking them down.

Gordon: Phew. Smells terrible. I bet there's rats down here.

Diane: There better hadn't be.

Gordon: We're near the river. There's always rats.

Diane: I don't wanna talk about it.

Gordon: Diane, look out, a rat!

Diane: Where ?!

Gordon: Only kidding.

Diane: You listen to me Gordon whatever-your-name-is, don't ever do that to me again! Got it?

(*Gordon looks surprised.*)

Gordon: OK. Sorry.

Diane: Who were those kids anyway? Friends of yours?

Gordon: No. I hate them. They're always hanging about waiting to get you.

Diane: They'd better not find this place. What is this, the cellars?

Gordon: Yeah. Bit creepy, eh? Ghoulies and ghosties, eh? Whooo!

Diane: Don't, I said! You believe in ghosts, then, do yer?

Gordon: No.

Diane: Well, I don't neither. So shut up about it. It smells like a toilet. Ugh! Look, everything's old. Like a prison.

Gordon: They probably put their kids down here.

Diane: Who?

Gordon: People who used to live here. Tied them up and left them when they were trouble. So the rats and spiders could crawl all over them.

Diane: Do you have to?

Gordon: You're scared!

Diane: I'm more scared of what'll happen if I get caught and taken back to the Home.

Gordon: What you scared of there, then?

Diane: There's these two girls there. They're after me, 'cos I can't keep me temper. I hit one once. So they're going to get me. So I packed up me supplies and ran for it.

(*She has pulled out a packet of crisps, which she starts to open and eat.*)

Gordon: Supplies? What for?

Diane: I'm leaving this country. Emigrating. Somewhere nice and warm. Africa, somewhere like that.

(*She offers him crisps.*)

Gordon: Africa? They'd never let you in.

Diane: No?

Gordon: No. Not a person from a Home. Anyway, you're too scared.

Diane: *You* are! You ran away!

Gordon: So? Anyway, I don't wanna go to Africa, do I?

Diane: We could stop here and make it a den.

Gordon: Urgh, no. Tramps use it.

Diane: So what?

Gordon: I can't stand tramps. They stink.

Diane: (*Hearing a noise.*) Sssshh! Listen! Gordon . . . I thought I heard something!

(*They both listen.*)

Diane: No. Thought someone was coming.

Gordon: Don't do that. My heart's going crazy.

(*They listen again for a moment. Relax and come to a stillness. Not a freeze but a relaxed, neutral position which the actors can hold comfortably.*)

1780s

(*Jacob jerks awake, as if woken by a sudden noise. He looks warily at the door.*)

Jacob: Issie?

(*Issie stirs.*)

Issie: Hnn? No! Don't hit me, please!

(*She's curled into a ball to protect herself.*)

Jacob: Issie, it's all right, it's all right.

(*He still looks out warily.*)

Jacob: It's me, Jacob.

Issie: (*Clinging to him.*) I was dreaming. Dreaming we were back home in Africa.

Jacob: No, we're still in this new . . . this cold place. We must forget about Africa.

(*As they talk, they groom each other, a joint ritual that they have decided on to try and keep their morale up.*)

Issie: Why? Forget Africa? Forget our home, forget mother and father, forget *everything*?

Jacob: We'll never see them again. You must learn that, Issie.

(*She is silent for a moment, then pulls at her chains, then Jacob's chains. She moves as far as she can around the cellar, as if to reproach Jacob, who sits at the other end of the chain.*)

Jacob: Forget, Issie!

(*Issie turns to address the audience.*)

Issie: For three days we have been in this terrible cold place they call Bristol, in England. My brother and me. His name is Olu, but the whiteghost sailors who brought us here called him Jacob. Now, he will not be Olu. He must be Jacob. *He* says. Soon, we will be sold to a whiteghost who makes sugar in the West Indies. We will be pushed into a ship, and if we arrive safely, we will be made to work until we die. If we don't work, then we will be killed. That is why I, Issie Mabofu, have decided I will not go. I will escape.

(*She goes to the window in the wall, stands on tiptoe, and peers out.*)

Jacob: Pardon?

Issie: What?

Jacob: I thought you said something?

Issie: No. Look, Jacob, people, whiteghosts, out there, walking up and down.

Jacob: Be quiet, Issie. If they hear you, the whiteghost master will come and beat us again.

Issie: (*Laughing.*) Look at this, Jacob, look!

Jacob: Look, look. You're always looking. You must stop, you must keep your eyes down now. We are in this terrible place, this England. We must make ourselves small as rats in the bush. Then perhaps we won't be beaten and killed.

Issie: I'm not listening to you, Jacob. (*Laughs.*) They have such fat bottoms, look!

(*She poses herself like a fat, rich lady, wearing a bustle.*)

Issie: Like a great rhinoceros. Oh, now there's some *poor* whiteghosts. Urgh! Poor creatures. They're bent over. Like sticks in the wind. They beg for food, Jacob, look! One has no leg. His face is white as death. Come up, come up and see. Poor people.

Jacob: Poor? You can't feel sorry for them. What about us?

Issie: While we have arms and legs and can work, then we are worth money to the whiteghost masters. They won't hurt us while they can get money for us. That beggar is worth nothing to them.

Jacob: And what happens when we are too old or ill to work for them? You're crazy! You may be my sister, but I say this to you, Issie, you are crazy! Sometimes I wish I were chained up to someone else, an animal, anybody! Anybody with a bit of sense in their head!

(*Issie is hurt by this. She slumps against the wall. Jacob realises he's said the wrong thing. He stands and goes to her.*)

Jacob: I'm sorry, Issie. That was wrong. You're my sister. I will always look after you.

Issie: I don't want you to look after me, Olu, I want us to escape!

Jacob: Escape? Ha! Where to?

Issie: Anywhere!

Jacob: We just take these off, do we?

(*He rattles the chain in her face.*)

Issie: I know, brother. I can feel them too.

(*She turns to look out of the window again.*)

Issie: The beggars have gone. Look, look Olu, more whiteghosts with big bottoms!

(*She calls him over and they both look. They giggle, and she does another imitation, walking up and down being fat and pompous. He sees someone, and does a matching impression, e.g. someone thin and bloodless, a vicar perhaps. They greet each other, bowing and scraping. All the time, their parodies are hindered by the chain. In the middle of this, which is accompanied by their laughter, Issie suddenly flops.*)

Issie: When will they give us something to eat?

Jacob: When they feel like it.

Issie: I wonder what will it be? Bread with maggots in? Or maggots with bread?

Jacob: Boiled maggots and bread?

Issie: Or bread, and boiled maggots?

Jacob: And a pan of dirty water, with . . . (*Stirs imaginary water with finger.*)

Issie:
Jacob: } (*Together.*) Dead maggots!

Issie: Oh don't. You're making me feel hungry.

Jacob: Sssshh.

(*They freeze.*)

Jacob: What was that?

Issie: I didn't hear anything.

Jacob: Thought I heard a sound.

Issie: No . . . listen.

Jacob: Down!

(*They huddle in the sacking like cowering animals, eyes fixed on the door. After a moment, they breathe easily again. They come to stillness.*)

1980s

Diane: No. There's no one there. Just don't want to get caught, that's all.

Gordon: You're daft, you know that?

Diane: Don't say things like that to me.

Gordon: Why not? It's a daft idea coming here. It's a daft idea bunking off from school. So why shouldn't I call you that?

Diane: Because I don't like it. Right?

Gordon: OK, OK. Keep your hair on!

(*He flicks her hair. She twists away angrily. He walks on round the space, prodding bits of rubbish with his foot.*)

Diane: It wasn't my idea.

Gordon: Whose was it then?

Diane: Yours as well.

Gordon: OK. So it was. But this is stupid. It stinks, it's freezing cold, and we're both scared to go outside in case there's police, or those older kids outside, waiting to get us. That's daft.

Diane: I'm not going, Gordon. Right?

Gordon: OK. Please yourself. (*Stands and looks around the cellar.*) What do you reckon this place was?

Diane: I dunno. Someone off the river lived here, I expect. Fisherman or something.

Gordon: No. Too big. It's vast, this place. It'd have to be someone rich, eh?

Diane: Live in a dump like this?

Gordon: It wasn't always a dump, was it? There'd be great big rooms upstairs, and servants, and featherbeds, and a great kitchen on the go day and night. You could send down for anything anytime.

Diane: Could yer?

Gordon: Sure! 'Send me up a dozen quarterpounders with french fries, and a hundred strawberry milkshakes. And be quick about it.' 'Oh, yes sir, straight away, sir.' And off he goes to the kitchens.

Diane: (*Starting to play the game.*) Who does?

Gordon: The butler.

Diane: What's his name?

Gordon: Er . . . Simpkins.

Diane: Simpkins?! Go on.

Gordon: So Simpkins goes down to the kitchens. And there'd be a great fire, with a grill, and a hundred hamburgers on the go . . .

(*As he talks, Diane's hands steal into her bag and start transporting crisps into her mouth.*)

. . . and fried onions on that side, and chips on that side, all sizzling, and two other servants mixing up the milkshakes on that side . . .

(*Diane has run out of crisps. She searches frantically for more, but can't find any. Gordon notices her, and the empty crisp-bag.*)

Gordon: Diane!

Diane: I'm hungry!

Gordon: So am I.

Diane: Well, stop talking about hamburgers . . .

Gordon: . . . and french fries?

Diane: . . . yes, and onions . . .

Gordon: . . . and milkshakes?

Diane: Stoppit!

Gordon: (*As Simpkins the butler.*) Yes, madam. Is there anything madam would require? A nice warm blanket to keep out the cold?

Diane: Yes. The extra-thick furry one, with gold thread in. And quick.

Gordon: Yes, madam, the extra-thick furry one, with gold in. Right away.

(*He picks up a piece of dusty sacking. Shakes it off, makes himself cough. Places it on her lap.*)

Gordon: There we are, madam.

Diane: Oh Simpkins (*Yawn.*) I've changed my mind. I want the extra-extra thick one, with diamonds round the edges. It is a little chilly tonight.

(*Gordon takes the sacking from her, turns it round and replaces it on her.*)

Diane: Ah, bliss. Have the next five minutes off, Simpkins.

Gordon: How kind, madam!

Diane: Yes I am. Now I'm going to sleep for a few minutes Gordon — er, Simpkins. I don't want *any* noise, do you hear?

Gordon: Yes, madam. You've got a snotty nose.

Diane: I beg your pardon?

Gordon: Yes, madam. I shall walk on tip-toes.

Diane: Good. See that you do.

(*She puts the sacking over her head and pretends to sleep. Gordon addresses the audience.*)

Gordon: This is stupid. I could just go off, eh? Well, it might be safer back in school than trapped down here. I don't want to spend all day in here, even if she does. (*Glances at Diane.*) Right. I'm off.

Diane: Gordon?

Gordon: What?

Diane: Who were you talking to?

Gordon: No one.

Diane: I want an ice-cream, Simpkins.

(*Gordon hesitates and shows audience his change of mind.*)

Gordon: Hey, wait a minute. You be the servant, eh?

Diane: No.

Gordon: Go on, I want a go.

Diane: I'm not being your slave.

Gordon: Why not? You've had your go.

Diane: You must be joking. You're not pushing me around.

Gordon: It's stupid, Diane. If you aren't going to play, then we might as well go back.

Diane: Back?

Gordon: School.

Diane: I'm not going back to the Home. I told you, I'm emigrating to Africa.

Gordon: How? Don't be stupid.

Diane: Stow away. On a ship.

Gordon: Oh yes? What about the people who look after you? At the Home.

Diane: They aren't coming.

Gordon: You know what I mean. They'll be worried.

Diane: So?

Gordon: So think about someone else for a change.

(*She gets up, discomforted. She goes to the door with the chalked drawings.*)

Diane: Look at this.

Gordon: It's kids.

Diane: Don't get it. What's it supposed to be?

Gordon: Looks like a story. Kind of cartoon.

Diane: More like grown-ups then. Kids just put their names.

(*She indicates the modern graffiti.*)

Gordon: What happens if the school rings up my mum and dad?

Diane: Gordon! Stop going on about it. Let them! I don't care!

(*They come to stillness.*)

1780s

(*Jacob gets up and goes to the door. He starts to draw a new picture on it.*)

Issie: And what use is that?

Jacob: I don't know. It pleases me. It's like telling a story.

Issie: There's no one to see it, except us. You're stupid.

Jacob: Someone might come to this place after us.

Issie: Jacob!

Jacob: We have to tell people what has happened to us.

Issie: Look!

Jacob: What?

Issie: By your foot.

Jacob: Mice. I know. The place is running with them.

Issie: No, look! That bowl by your foot.

(*Jacob looks down to find a bowl of food. It is thin soup and stale bread.*)

Jacob: You're right! How long's that been there?

Issie: The whiteghosts must have put it there in the night.

(*Jacob carefully brings the food over to Issie. They are both very hungry, but reluctant to start on it in case it disappears.*)

Issie: Don't spill any!

Jacob: I won't!

(*Issie takes a piece of bread. Jacob also takes a piece, and is about to eat it when —*)

Issie: Wait!

Jacob: What?

Issie: Why are they giving us food? They must want our strength up. That means we're going to be sold soon.

(*Jacob is again about to eat when —*)

Issie: They may want to split us up, Jacob. If we're to escape, we'll have to do it soon. (*Looks at him.*) Well, eat up! We're going to need all our strength.

(*Jacob gratefully eats. So does Issie. They eat slowly, eyes closed.*)

Issie: Mmmm . . . chicken!

Jacob: Chicken?

Issie: You try. Close your eyes.

(*She gives him a piece of bread.*)

Jacob: Mmmm . . . pineapple . . .

Issie: Mmmm . . . goat's milk cheese . . .

Jacob: Mmmm . . . fufu . . . cashew nuts . . .

Issie: Mmmm . . . palm leaves and dates . . .

Jacob: Mmmm . . .

(*He puts his hands down for more, but it's gone. Opens his eyes.*)

Jacob: Where's the last bit?

Issie: What bit?

Jacob: It was mine. You took it!

Issie: I did not. It's all gone. They don't want us to feel *too* strong, remember.

Jacob: I was thinking of the last time we ate together, you and me and mother and father. Before the whiteghosts.

Issie: You shouted at me. You said I'd taken your last piece of chicken.

Jacob: My bowl was suddenly empty.

Issie: But it wasn't me. Father had taken it, and hidden it behind his back.

Jacob: And you pretended you didn't know.

Issie: And you got so *angry*! Your eyes wide, Jacob, and your arms waving like trees in the wind. And tears . . . oh!

Jacob: Then father showed me the piece of chicken. And he laughed and laughed.

Issie: And mother had to give you more pineapple to stop you crying.

Jacob: Nothing wrong with that. It was a bad trick to play on me.

Issie: Yes it was. Poor old Olu!

Jacob: No tricks here, though. No chicken either. Just old bread and bone.

(*He stands and moves to the door.*)

Issie: What are you going to do?

Jacob: More of the story. Us all together. In the village.

(*Jacob starts to draw his picture on the door. Issie starts to sing a song from her home. She throws out suggestions as she does so: '. . . Now some trees . . . now the goat . . .', etc. Finally '. . . now show the whiteghosts.' Jacob finds he cannot do it.*)

Issie: The day the whiteghosts took us away, Jacob.

(*She turns out. It's as if we're seeing the pictures that flash through their minds in an instant. Jacob turns out.*)

Issie: Afternoon. Great clouds, white on the mountains, like a giant's hat.

Jacob: No wind. Birds playing in the sky.

Issie: Goats and children playing in the village dust.

Jacob: Very quiet.

Issie: Very quiet. You and me playing Throw-stones in the dust.

(*They start to play jacks with something they've found in the rubbish on the floor.*)

Jacob: We waved goodbye to mother and father who went to the next village.

Issie: They took medicine they had made to a friend who was ill.

Jacob: We waved, and they waved back.

Issie: That was the last time ever we saw them.

Jacob: Them waving, and us waving back. We played for a bit more. Then we saw that the birds had gone out of the sky. It was silent.

Issie: All around the village were white ghosts. White faces. A white tribe we had never seen before.

Jacob: We thought: Had they come from the white moon?

Issie: They wore thick clothes and looked hot.

Jacob: Some had feathers in their hats and looked like peacocks.

Issie: They all had iron in their hands. To put on our necks and arms and legs.

Jacob: Iron to hurt, iron to kill.

Issie: Iron to drag us away from our village, and our houses, and our land.

Jacob: Away from the trees and the goats, and the mountains, with the white clouds on the top, like a giant's hat.

Issie: Leaving behind our village, with the dead bodies of those who had tried to stop the whiteghosts.

Jacob: So that was what mother and father would have seen, when they came back.

Issie: Their children gone, just the empty village, and the great mountains with white clouds on the top, like a giant's hat.

Jacob: How can I draw all that?

(*He throws the chalk down and gives up.*)

Issie: Remember the song? Remember what mother taught us?

(*She starts to sing.*)

Issie: Remember?

(*Jacob joins in.*)

Issie: As long as we sing this, Jacob, we won't forget mother and father. We ... won't forget them waving to us.

(*She stands up and goes to the window. She sings out of that. Jacob is alarmed and stops singing.*)

Jacob: Sssh! Issie! Stop! They'll hear us!

Issie: Yes, Jacob. They'll hear us out in the street, and down the river, and out across the sea. They'll hear us in Africa!

(*She sings more.*)

Jacob: Sssh! Issie! We'll be beaten!

(*He tries to stop her by pulling on the chain. She is pulled away from the window, but goes to the door instead, and sings through it.*)

Jacob: Issie, I'm scared, I'm scared!

Issie: Don't be, Olu. Let's fill their cold house with our Africa!

(*Jacob tries to stop her by putting his hand over her mouth. She pushes him away. Suddenly they both freeze. It's as if the door has suddenly opened, and they react as if being beaten to the ground. They come to stillness, huddled in the sacking.*)

1980s

Gordon: How would you like it, eh? If you suddenly found your mum and dad had gone when you got home?

Diane: Wouldn't bother me. Shut up about it. Look at these . . .

(*Diane starts to sing Issie's song as she peers at the pictures.*)

Gordon: Sounds like there's a rat caught in the drains.

Diane: Where? Urgh!

Gordon: No, it's stopped now.

(*She carries on singing to herself.*)

Gordon: There it goes again. Sounds like it's in agony.

Diane: Funny, funny.

Gordon: What is it, anyway, that song?

Diane: I dunno. Never heard it before.

(*She carries on singing.*)

Gordon: Then how can you sing it if you've never heard it?

Diane: I . . . I don't know, do I? Stop getting at me.

Gordon: I'm cold.

Diane: (*Referring to the pictures.*) I wonder what these are? What's it mean?

Gordon: Nothing. It's just kids mucking about. What do you reckon the time is?

Diane: How do I know? Look at this. Looks like they started this one and never finished it. It's some kind of . . . there's trees . . .

Gordon: It's rubbish! I can draw better than that.

Diane: . . . sun . . . some people . . . they're all joined together, look Gordon, look . . .

Gordon: It's a dance. Some kind of disco.

Diane: Wally!

Gordon: This is boring. Let's go.

Diane: I wanna look at this.

Gordon: Hey, why don't we go down the amusements?

Diane: What for?

Gordon: Play the videos. Give you a game of Fighter Patrol. I'm great at that. (*Machine-gun noises.*)

Diane: Oh, that'll be fun for me, won't it?

Gordon: Oh come on!

(*He goes to the drawings. Picks up a bit of sacking and tries to rub the drawings out. Diane grabs his arm and pulls him away from the wall.*)

Gordon: Don't touch me!

Diane: Don't touch those pictures, then!

Gordon: What's it to you? It's only kids!

Diane: I like them. All right?

Gordon: What if I don't?

Diane: I don't care!

Gordon: What if *I* say *I* don't like them?

Diane: You would, wouldn't you?

Gordon: What do you mean?

Diane: Too scared to go to school, so you take it out on some kids' drawings.

Gordon: The kids aren't going to care, are they? They're not here, are they?

Diane: I don't know. They might be very near, actually.

Gordon: Well, don't let them come near me, or I'll kick their heads in.

Diane: Yes, you would.

(*Pause. Gordon picks up a piece of sacking. Diane tenses.*)

Diane: Gordon!

Gordon: It's OK. I won't touch your precious pictures.

Diane: Good. Are you sure you haven't anything else to eat?

Gordon: What?

Diane: Simpkins!

Gordon: Yes, madam?

Diane: I'm hungry.

Gordon: Again, your ladyship?

Diane: Again, Simpkins. I require a little snack.

Gordon: Ummm . . . a sausage roll, madam?

Diane: Very good, Simpkins.

(*Gordon pokes about in the rubbish. Finds a dead mouse. Wraps it in a piece of paper or sacking.*)

Diane: Hurry up, man, I'm starving.

Gordon: Coming right away, madam.

(*She smoothes a place on her lap. Gordon lays the parcel there.*)

Diane: Ah, delightful. (*She starts up.*) Oh, Gordon! Get it off, it's disgusting!

(*He waves it about in front of her. She, however, reacts bored, not hysterical as he had hoped.*)

Diane: You'll get diseases off it. Fleas!

(*Gordon is suddenly worried by that. He stops waving the mouse about, and rather gingerly throws it away. Wipes his fingers obsessively on his trousers.*)

Gordon: When can we go, Diane?

Diane: Soon, all right? I just wanna explore a bit more.

(*She finds a bit of stick and pokes about in the rubbish with it.*)

Gordon: I think I'm going anyway. I'm fed up in here.

Diane: OK then. I'm not bothered.

Gordon: Won't you be scared being on your own?

Diane: Scared?

(*She shrugs, as if to say she will be. She pokes about a bit more fiercely, then finds something.*)

Diane: Hey, look!

(*She fishes out a bunch of old and rusty keys.*)

Gordon: What's that?

Diane: Bunch of keys, what's it look like?

Gordon: Let's see.

(*She pulls the keys away from him. They play a game of him trying to get the keys. Eventually she shoots the keys off the end of the stick towards him. They spread them out to look at them.*)

Gordon: They look old.

Diane: Must be part of the house.

Gordon: Take 'em to the museum. Might be worth something!

Diane: We could *give* them to the museum. Get our names on a label.

Gordon: Get our names on a label? Big deal! I'd rather have the money.

Diane: Wonder what they're for?

Gordon: Opening things.

Diane: Clever, clever. Opening what things?

Gordon: Doors. That door perhaps? Or that chain thing up there.

(*He finds a bit of chain with a wrist manacle on. He tries it on.*)

Diane: Careful, Gordon. Don't muck about.

Gordon: What'd happen if you got chained up in here? No one'd ever hear you. You'd starve to death. Or they'd bulldoze the whole place on top of you. Squashed flat — strawberry jam.

Diane: Do you have to?

Gordon: Dare me?

Diane: Don't be stupid.

Gordon: Do you?

Diane: Don't, Gordon.

(*He clicks the manacle on to his wrist. Diane looks on appalled.*)

Diane: You nutter! You'll have to stay like that now!

Gordon: One of those keys'll open it.

Diane: How do you know?

Gordon: Try it.

Diane: Maybe.

Gordon: Oh, come on, Diane.

Diane: What if I don't?

Gordon: I'll tell the Home where you are.

Diane: You won't be able to. You'll be stuck down here, won't you?

Gordon: Oh come on, Diane. Don't mess about.

Diane: Say please.

Gordon: Please.

Diane: Say: Diane's the most brilliant thing ever in the whole world.

Gordon: Diane's the most stupid − brilliant thing in the whole world.

Diane: And Gordon's a slimy toad with smelly feet.

(*Silence.*)

Diane: Come on, or you'll stay there.

Gordon: Gordon's a slimy toad with smelly feet.

Diane: Better.

Gordon: Come on then, you promised.

Diane: Did I? Oh.

Gordon: I thought we were helping each other.

Diane: Don't touch those pictures then. Promise.

Gordon: OK. I said I wouldn't.

Diane: Promise.

Gordon: Promise. What's so special about them all of a sudden?

Diane: I don't know, do I? They just are, that's all. Give us your hand then.

(*She tries out the keys, finds the right one, and unlocks him.*)

Gordon: Great. Now can we go?

Diane: OK. Let's see what else we can find to take with us.

Gordon: There's only rubbish.

Diane: But we found the keys. Might be other things.

Gordon: You're trouble — you know that?

(*She squats down on the floor, looking.*)

Diane: Gimme a hand, then.

(*He squats down too. They come to stillness.*)

1780s

(*Jacob and Issie stir, and get up painfully. They have been beaten.*)

Jacob: What did I tell you? We sing — the Whiteghosts beat us. I told you, I warned you. You're trouble, do you know that? Trouble. No good, Issie.

Issie: At least we know they heard us. It's not that bad. Is it?

(*He stretches himself and winces.*)

Jacob: Yes, it is.

(*She rubs her bruises.*)

Issie: Yes ... perhaps you're right. But they did hear us. Up there in their cold house where they buy and sell. That makes my bruises feel better.

Jacob: Not mine. Those whiteghosts, they aren't hurt when we sing. They're just like the hunter who beats his dog for howling in the night.

Issie: But we're not dogs, and we show the whiteghosts that by singing.

Jacob: We should do as we're told. They'll treat us better.

Issie: No they won't. They'll still sell us to the sugar farmers. They'll still work us till we die. No. I'm for singing.

(*She sings.*)

Jacob: Issie, please!

(*She takes pity on him and stops.*)

Issie: I'm only singing for mother and father. One day we'll go back to Africa. One day we'll see them again.

Jacob: You're dreaming. What about these?

(*He rattles the chain.*)

Issie: We won't be chained up when we're working.

Jacob: They kill slaves who run away. I told you, you've gone mad. And if you could escape, what then? How are you going to get back to Africa? Buy a ticket on a whiteghost ship? We'll never see Africa again, and we might as well admit it.

Issie: Well I won't admit it. If we make enough trouble for them, it won't be worth them having slaves. They'd have to find some other way of getting sugar.

Jacob: Huh! You think they'd cut it themselves? Can you imagine that?

(*He does an impression of a posh whiteghost, prissily cutting cane in the sun.*)

Issie: (*Laughing.*) They'll think up some magic. They'll have to if they want their sugar and their money.

Jacob: And if you escape here? You're a black slave in a white land.

Issie: Some of them would help us. Some of those beggars out there, the sticks in the wind, they'd help us. They're no better than slaves.

Jacob: We have to stay together, you and me.

Issie: Of course. You can come with me.

Jacob: No. It's not possible. The best we can hope for is that some rich whiteghost will take us on as their personal servants. It's a good life if you learn to do as you're told.

Issie: Good life?!

Jacob: Issie, rest now. Don't let's waste our strength in fighting each other.

(*Issie fumes. Jacob lets his eyes close.*)

Jacob: Rest, Issie. Rest . . .

(*She can't. She has seen the bunch of keys left on the floor by Diane. Issie's face lights up.*)

Issie: Jacob . . .

Jacob: No more arguments! Rest, I said.

(*He dozes. Issie waits for a minute. She tries to reach for the keys. Can't do it. She keeps trying. The rattling and tugging of the chain wakes Jacob.*)

Jacob: Wha . . .? What're you doing *now*?

Issie: Look, Jacob, look.

(*She keeps trying to reach for the keys, but the chain restricts her.*)

Jacob: Look, look, look! Always *looking*. Trouble!

Issie: There! Those keys!

Jacob: Oh. Where did they come from?

Issie: I don't know. They must have been hidden by the darkness and the dirt. The whiteghosts have forgotten about them. Who cares where they came from? Now let this chain out a bit, will you?

Jacob: Why?

Issie: Why? They might unlock us, of course.

Jacob: You don't know that. Locks and keys are whiteghost
magic. They never do what you expect them to do.

Issie: Let's try at least. Stop holding me in!

Jacob: And what if they do unlock us? What then?

Issie: Then we're at the start of our great escape!

Jacob: No, no. It's too dangerous.

Issie: I want the keys.

Jacob: No.

Issie: Jacob!

Jacob: No! I said no. Think of mother and father.

Issie: I am. We must get back to them.

Jacob: They would want us to stay alive and well. Not take
risks with our lives.

(*Issie keeps trying to stretch out to them, but Jacob stops her.*)

Issie: You've *got* to help me. I'm your sister.

Jacob: If you escaped, I'd never see you again. I wouldn't *have*
a sister!

(*Issie keeps trying but can't reach them. She relaxes. Jacob drifts
off. Issie decides to try another tactic. She uses a piece of stick, or
similar, and starts carefully and quietly to pull the keys to her.
They both come to stillness.*)

1980s

Diane: Found anything?

Gordon: No.

Diane: Nor me. Just dirt.

Gordon: It's getting dark. Can't see so well. We ought to go.

Diane: OK, OK. Let's take the keys with us.

Well, give them to me.

Gordon: What?

Diane: The keys. They were on the floor.

Gordon: I haven't got them.

Diane: You have. I know you. You'll go down to that museum place and try to sell them. Come on, Gordon.

Gordon: Honest!

Diane: They were here a minute ago. Now they've gone. So where are they?

Gordon: Don't ask me. I don't want that old rubbish.

Diane: Oh, come on Gordon, please. Don't mess about.

Gordon: For the last time, I have not got your keys!

Diane: I don't believe you.

Gordon: The sooner we get out of here the better.

Diane: What do you mean?

Gordon: Vanishing keys, funny noises, singing songs you've never heard of. I'm starting to think you're going potty down here. Next thing you'll be telling me you're seeing ghosts.

1780s

(*They come to stillness. Issie continues slowly, quietly, to 'fish' in the keys to her. It takes a very long time. Very gingerly, she retrieves them and unlocks herself. Jacob stirs but doesn't wake. Slowly she stands, freed, rubbing her wrists.*)

Issie: Jacob.

(*He stirs.*)

Issie: Look.

Jacob: What? (*He sees her and starts up.*) Now what have you done?

Issie: It's easy. Free yourself.

(*She offers the keys to him.*)

Jacob: How did you . . . ?

Issie: Because I *wanted* to. Now you.

Jacob: No.

Issie: You must. It works. Look!

Jacob: You'll never get away with it, Issie.

Issie: I must try, Jacob.

(*She tries the keys in the door. The lock opens.*)

Issie: See? It's open, Jacob.

Jacob: I'm scared.

Issie: So am I. But I must go.

Jacob: Go on, then.

Issie: Come with me.

Jacob: It's dangerous.

Issie: It's dangerous to stay.

Jacob: Where will you go?

Issie: To a place they call London. There are black people there.

Jacob: Living? Not slaves?

Issie: Yes. There've always been black people in this England. They will shelter me.

Jacob: You cannot go on your own.

Issie: And you cannot stop me!

(*A pause. Jacob is torn. Finally, he puts out his wrists to be unlocked. Issie unlocks him. The chains now all lie on the floor. Issie grips him by the arms.*)

Jacob: Wait. There's one more thing we have to do.

(*He goes to the door and starts to add a final image. It is a figure who has broken his chains.*)

Jacob: In case we don't get to Africa. So somebody will know about us.

(*He gathers up bits of sacking for the journey. They embrace quickly.*)

Issie: Good luck, Olu.

Olu: Good luck, Issie.

(*Issie tries out keys, one by one, trying not to make noise. One works, and she carefully pushes the door open.*)

Issie: Ssssh. Whiteghosts. (*She listens.*) OK.

(*She leaves the room first. Olu has one last anxious look round the room, then leaves, pulling the door closed after him.*)

1980s

Diane: What was that?

Gordon: What?

Diane: That sound.

Gordon: Only the door. It's the wind. It's getting cold and dark.

Diane: Gordon . . .

Gordon: Now what?

Diane: Look. That drawing.

Gordon: I've seen 'em. Come on, let's go.

Diane: No look, there's a new one. Did you do it?

Gordon: Me? I can draw better than that. I'm not a kid playing with chalk, y'know. Spraycan artist, me. (*Mimes it.*)

Diane: Well, it wasn't there before, and I didn't do it.

Gordon: Of course it was there before. Stop wasting time, will you? Are we going back now, or what?

Diane: Might as well. Can't be scared all the time.

Gordon: OK. We coming back here?

Diane: (*Looking round the cellar.*) Me? No. It's empty now.

Gordon: You scared?

Diane: Me? No. You?

Gordon: No.

Diane: Come on, then.

(*Issie and Olu arrive on the road outside, with sacking wrapped round them.*)

Olu: Out on the road. Cold, dark.

Issie: Heart going thump, thump. Scared. But free.

(*Diane and Gordon arrive. They look about them.*)

Diane: Dark outside on the street. Cold.

Gordon: Streetlight gone out. Heart going thump. Listening in the dark.

Issie: Ready?

Olu: I'm ready, Issie.

Diane: Far off, lights at the end of the road.

Gordon: Looking out for kids, or police.

Issie: In the distance, lights from houses.

Olu: Hoping all the whiteghosts are asleep in bed.

Diane: Just then — thought I heard something —

Gordon: Something close by, someone near —

(*Issie starts quietly to sing her song.*)

Olu: We started to sing to keep our courage up.

(*Olu starts to sing.*)

Issie: Just then — thought I heard something — Whiteghosts? Nearby?

(*Diane starts to sing the song.*)

Gordon: Whoever it was, they've gone. Thought about tomorrow. What's going to happen to us all tomorrow?

He joins in the song. All four sing together. Then the two couples, who have been mingling, although not visible to each other, separate into their pairs and move off in different directions, still quietly singing.

Activities

Whiteghosts is a play for the stage. Before you put on a classroom performance, work through these exercises.

Thinking about the characters

Gordon

1 Gordon is bunking off from school. He says: 'I'm scared of school.' What do you think he means — the lessons? the rules? the other pupils? the teachers? Talk about why people play truant from school. In pairs, role-play a scene in which Gordon explains either to Diane or another of his friends why he is afraid of school.

2 What ideas about Gordon, his home and family did you develop as you read the play? Imagine you are going to play the part of Gordon. Write about yourself, your home, your family, your interests and your feelings about school. Then, form groups and compare your ideas about Gordon with other people's ideas about him.

3 Talk about how Gordon behaves while he and Diane are in the cellar.

a) Is he more scared or less scared than Diane? Quote evidence from the play to support your view.

b) Why does he get fed up of being in the cellar sooner than Diane does?

c) What do you think of the way he treats Diane and of the way he reacts to what she says and does?

Diane

1 Diane is running away from the Home. Discuss what she tells us about why she is running away. Then, imagine you are Diane and write about your feelings explaining why you are in the Home, why you are unhappy there and why you have decided to run away.

2 Talk about how Diane behaves while she and Gordon are in the cellar.

a) What is her attitude towards the cellar and the things in it? How far is it the same as Gordon's? How far is it different from Gordon's? Explain why.

b) What do you learn about Diane from what she says and does, and from the way she treats Gordon?

3 Near the end of the play, Diane says: 'Can't be scared all the time.' Talk about how their experiences in the cellar help Diane and Gordon to face up to their fears.

Issie and Jacob

1 Talk about the situation Issie and Jacob are in. What do they say and do which shows just how much they are missing their home?

2 If Issie and Jacob were able to send a short message home to their parents — the length of the message you can fit on to a postcard — what do you think they would write? Imagine you are Issie or Jacob. Write the message you would send.

3 Issie and her brother react differently to their situation. Olu says he is now called Jacob and that they must try to forget Africa. But Issie won't do so. Talk about why she won't listen to Jacob and why she insists that they must try to escape. Is Issie's plan 'crazy'? If you had been Jacob would you have agreed to go along with her? Give your reasons.

Thinking about the situations

Further developments

1 In pairs, role-play interviews with a) Diane, b) Gordon in which you ask them to explain why they ran away and to talk about their experience in the cellar. Before you begin, plan the interviews by working out a set of questions to ask them.

2 What will happen next? Will Gordon and Diane remain mates or will they just go their separate ways? Role-play a scene a few days later when, either by chance or by arrangement, Gordon and Diane meet again. Before you begin, decide what has happened to them since they were in the cellar. For example, what happened to Diane when she went back to the Home? Did Gordon get into trouble for bunking off school? Has he had to face any further name-calling incidents?

3 What will happen to Issie and Jacob alone and half-starving in a strange city? Imagine that they have met someone who has offered to help them. The person has told them to stay where they are and that he will return in half an hour. Once he has gone, they discuss whether or not they can trust him. Should they wait for his return or should they move on? One of them thinks they should wait, but the other thinks they should move on.

Parallel situations

1 In the play Diane says: 'Funny how quick you can be mates with someone you've never met.' Role-play a scene in which two children, like Diane and Gordon, suddenly find themselves running away or hiding together.

2 How would you feel if some strangers suddenly arrived at your home and took you away to be their slave? In pairs, imagine you are two children who, like Issie and Jacob, have been kidnapped, beaten, thrown into the hold of a ship and transported to a faraway country. Role-play a scene in which you talk about what has happened to you and tell each other about how much you miss your home. One of you, like Jacob, thinks you should try to make the best of your new situation. The other, like Issie, is determined to escape.

3 Talk about the master/servant game that Diane and Gordon play. How does the game mirror what has been happening to them in real life? What do you think they learn from playing the game? Try it yourself. In pairs, role-play a number of master/servant situations, taking it in turn to be the master and the servant. Then, talk about what it feels like a) when you are the master, b) when you are the servant.

4 At the start of the play, Gordon runs away because a group of children are calling him names. Role-play a scene in which a group of children are picking on someone and calling her/him names. At the point when the victim is about to run off, freeze in the positions you have adopted. One by one, take it in turns to try to express what your character is thinking and feeling at that point. Compare how the bullies are feeling with how the victim is feeling.

Presenting the play

1 When you are putting on a play, set in a different time or a different country, it is worth trying to find out as much as you can about that time or that place. For example, the more you know about the slave trade and slave ships, the more you will be able to understand exactly how Issie and Jacob must have felt and the more accurately you will be able to portray their feelings on stage. Using the resources in your school and local library, find out all you can about the slave trade in the eighteenth century. Note: One useful source of information about slave ships is Paula Fox's *The Slave Dancer* (Macmillan M Books).

2 Because *Whiteghosts* is set in a dingy, old cellar you could stage a production of it without having to make any elaborate scenery. But one thing you will have to decide is what the pictures that Jacob drew looked like and what piece of scenery you are going to draw them on. Remember the pictures do not need to be very artistic. Jacob, like many other people throughout history, is using symbols to portray his life-history rather than attempting to create a great work of art.

3 Another decision you must make is about Issie's song. Before you decide whether to look for a traditional African song or to try to write some words and music of your own, think carefully about the type of song she sings and why she sings it. The song expresses her longing to be back in Africa and helps her to remember her home and family. But it is also a song of defiance. She knows she will be beaten if she sings it, but that does not stop her. The song is something that cannot be taken away from her. It is something too that survives the centuries. So the play ends with all four children singing it, bound together by the sense of strength and unity which it gives.

Writing your own scripts

1 Using the information you learned from your research into the conditions on slave ships, write an extra scene to include in the play, in which Issie and Jacob talk about their journey from Africa to England. Present the conversation in the same way as the conversation about 'the day the whiteghosts took us away' is presented in the play.

2 a) Study the first scene of the play. Notice how, during this scene, Tony Coult makes both Diane and Gordon turn and address remarks directly to the audience. He uses this technique in order to enable them to tell the audience important facts about the situation that would not arise naturally in the conversations between them. Where else in the play does he use this technique?

b) Write a short script of your own about two children who are running away and hiding for some reason. At some point in your script use the technique of getting the characters to speak directly to the audience.

3 *Whiteghosts* tells two stories — one set in the 1980s, the other set in the 1780s. The author does this by setting the events of both stories in the same place and by limiting the number of characters involved, so that they can all be on stage throughout the play. Discuss the structure of the play and look again at the points in the play where the action shifts from the 1980s to the 1780s and from the 1780s to the present.

Notice how at the end of each scene there is a point of stillness, so that the two actors can relax into a neutral position, which they can hold while the other two actors develop their part of the plot.

Try to write a script of your own in which you use a similar technique. Either develop an idea of your own or use one of these ideas:

a) A play set in an air-raid shelter involving two children from today and two children from the 1940s.

b) A play set in an attic involving two children from today and two Victorian children.

c) A play set in a castle dungeon involving two children from the present and two people from medieval times.